John J. Geer

BEYOND THE LINES:

OR

A Yankee Prisoner Loose in Dixie.

BY CAPTAIN J. J. GEER,
LATE OF GENERAL BUCKLAND'S STAFF.

WITH AN INTRODUCTION,
BY REV. ALEXANDER CLARK.

"In the dark fens of the dismal swamp
The hunted Yankees lay;
They saw the fire of the midnight camp,
And heard at times the horses' tramp,
And the bloodhounds' distant bay."

PHILADELPHIA:
J. W. DAUGHADAY, PUBLISHER,
1308 CHESTNUT STREET.
1863.

PREFACE.

IN presenting the following narrative of suffering endured while a prisoner in the so-called Southern Confederacy, the principal object had in view by the author, is to place before those into whose hands this volume may come, a plain, straightforward, unvarnished account of *facts*.

In regard to the workings and results of that system of human bondage to which our country owes its present difficulties, there have been so many mistaken ideas, statements, and theories, that it has become the duty of every true and loyal man to expose the truth; or, speaking with more correctness, to strip from the hideous skeleton of Slavery all its gaily painted and deceptive cloaks and masks, and to exhibit it in all its ghastly repulsiveness.

It is my purpose in the succeeding pages to narrate simply how, after being captured at the battle of Shiloh, or Pittsburg Landing, I was, on the most frivolous charges, tried for my life before several prominent Rebel Generals, among whom were Bragg and Beauregard; how I was subsequently chained with negro chains and cast into military prisons and common jails; how, escaping from these, and in company with Lieutenant A. P. COLLINS, I made my way to the swamps; how we lived in these malarious marshes for three weeks; how we were hunted with bloodhounds; how we were assisted by the slaves in our flight, and lastly, how, being recaptured, we spent weary months in confinement, and were finally released on exchange from our dreadful captivity.

To all those friends who have cheered him since his return home with kind words and deeds, the author begs leave to extend his warmest thanks,—but more especially to Rev. ALEXANDER CLARK, Editor of *Clark's School Visitor*, who revised and arranged the Manuscripts for the press, and to whose scholarly abilities this volume owes so much. He desires also to testify to like kindness on the part of Rev. W. B. WATKINS, A. M., and MILO A. TOWNSEND, Esq., of New Brighton, Pennsylvania, whose friendship has laid him under a debt of grateful remembrance.

J. J. GEER.

SPRINGFIELD, OHIO, *June* 8, 1863.

TABLE OF CONTENTS.

CHAPTER I.

CHAPTER II.

CHAPTER III.

CHAPTER IV.

CHAPTER V.

CHAPTER VI.

CHAPTER VII.

CHAPTER VIII.

CHAPTER IX.

CHAPTER X.

CHAPTER XI.

CHAPTER XII.

CHAPTER XIII.

CHAPTER XIV.

CHAPTER XV.

CHAPTER XVI.

CHAPTER XVII.

CHAPTER XVIII.

CHAPTER XIX.

INTRODUCTION.

JOHN JAMES GEER was born in Rockbridge county, Virginia, June 1st, 1833. He is next to the youngest of a family of nine children. The father emigrated to Ohio when John was quite young, and settled in Shelby county, where he lived and labored as an industrious farmer for a long lifetime. Being in moderate circumstances, he was unable to educate his children as he wished, as their young hands were an indispensable help in the clearing and tilling of the land; but the lads wrought for themselves a training and discipline in the fields and at the fireside, such as made honest-hearted heroes of them.

Though this tuition may not be the most fashionable, it is far from being the least useful or influential in a nation like ours. The only external polish that will never grow coarse is the out-shining of inward purity and kindness. The law of love is a sufficient code of politeness and etiquette. The rarest soul-furnishing, and the most radiant and reliable loyalty, are virtuous intelligence, an appreciation of the true and the beautiful in Nature, in mind and morals, the utterance of generous impulses, the self-respect that prefers its own calm approval to the world's admiration and flattery. Such a heroism is purely democratic, and sets the price of its integrity too high to offer itself as a prize for party bidding! It stands like a granite pillar, strong, and straight, and upright. We may build on this, and stand secure for solid years. It is this untrammeled life the nation needs at this very time in the hearts of all her citizens.

Mr. Geer never received any lessons in the school of pretences. He never learned the art of deceiving or being deceived. He studied something deeper of the world while his hands held the plough that furrowed its surface. He gained more instruction from the leaves on the forest trees than from the leaves of printed books. He cultivated at one and the same time his own mind, and the soil of his father's farm. His surroundings were the pictures and poetries of Nature. His eye saw no shams, his ear heard no complaints, his heart knew no hypocrisies. Trained in such a school, he became a thinker and a worker; his associations were altogether with plain and practical people; he was never flushed with feverish fancies, nor discouraged at any disappointments. Always cheerful, as only a busy doer and darer can be, he grew into manhood, full-built, tough-muscled, keen-nerved, and strong-minded. He acquired by hygienic habits a "constitution" that needed never an "amendment." He shaped, all unconsciously to himself, a moral character as honorable as it was humble; yet it was such as recognized in the minutest particular, and exacted to the fullest degree, the claims of a common brotherhood.

Pure democracy, like all living, blossoming, fruit-bearing growths, flourishes best in the country. A principle that strikes root in an hour in the hotbed of the city, is apt to wilt and die in the sunshine of the open world. Aristocracy may be plaited into politics; but it takes integrity and fellow-hood for web and woof of republicanism. Young Geer was a democrat, in the honest signification of the term. Though poor and sunburnt, hard-fisted and plain-worded, he learned to feel that no man in the republic was his superior in rights—that no man in the republic was his inferior in privileges. The truth of Holy Writ, that declares "all nations to be of one blood," was his confession of faith in conscience and Christianity. The spirit of the Declaration of Independence, that "all men are created free and equal," was his political platform. These high authorities gave him early and earnest boldness as a friend of human liberty.

At the age of eighteen, he was called to the work of the Gospel ministry. He passed into this work, not as a mere *profession*, by the paths marked out by ecclesiastics,—not by college carpets and seminary shades,—but as the early preachers were called, so was he, from his daily avocation. His inherent firmness made him an unyielding, if not an aggressive Christian. He stemmed a strong current of opposition from the beginning of his ministry. His independent manner gave offence to rowdy transgressors, and frequently was he threatened and waylaid by the very doers of the deeds he made it a business to denounce in his sermons. But he wavered not from his sense of duty.

One of his first and truest friends was the Rev. R. M. DALBY, a well-known minister and Temperance reformer in South-western Ohio. These two men were acknowledged leaders in the war of annihilation against King Alcohol and his conscripted hosts. For years they were joined in word and work in the good cause of Temperance, and were separated only when, in the spring of 1861, Geer heard his wounded country's cry for help, and quickly stepped to a place in the front rank of her brave defenders. His well-tried associate in battling against wrong, Mr. Dalby, was left behind now, only because he was physically unable to march to the rescue.

Before entering the army of the Union, Mr. Geer had spent some ten years in the ministry, in and around the city of Cincinnati. During that time he received about eleven hundred members into the church. He was eminently successful as a revivalist. When Fort Sumpter was fired upon, he was stationed as pastor of the George Street Methodist Protestant Church, in Cincinnati. When the news of the outrage was received at the Queen City, the pastor of George Street Church vowed he was a United States soldier until either himself or the rebellion should be crushed. He began recruiting at once for the Army of Freedom, and was as successful as he had been in marshaling forces for the Army of Peace.

Until this time he had been unwilling to interfere with the "peculiar institution" of the South. But the moment the Stars and Stripes were insulted by the proud power, that moment a new resolve was made, to hate and to hurt the accursed thing henceforward, until the last vestige of it should be obliterated from American soil!

Captain Geer is an earnest man. He engaged in the war, not for position or popularity, but as a soldier. Although he started into the service as Chaplain, he was willing to resign that responsible office to the charge of another; and at once accepted a position that promised more excitement and adventure in days of battle. He was appointed Assistant-Adjutant General on the Staff of General Buckland, which commission he held when he was wounded and captured at Shiloh.

In these days of adventure and sacrifice, when the noblest men in the nation are made to suffer for country's sake, it is shameful to see how certain northern people and papers, professing to be loyal, are in sympathy with the arch treason of the Secessionists. However well-attested may be the statements of surviving sufferers,—and no matter how fair the reputation of the man who dares to denounce the Slaveholders' Rebellion,—there are lurking copperheads with viper tongues to hiss their venomous abuses on all the brave soldiers who have bled under the Federal banner! From the liberty to talk treason, slander the Administration, and abuse the soldiers—O God, deliver us! The nation cries for *liberty*—not license—a liberty that is always loyal to God and this

Government—a liberty to love and bless the poor, the outcast, the suffering, and the oppressed!

It may not be amiss to append the following extracts from letters which will explain themselves:

"SPRINGFIELD, OHIO, MAY 3, 1863.

"*To all whom it may concern:*—

"The undersigned, ministers of the Gospel in the Methodist Protestant Church, take pleasure in certifying that Captain John J. Geer is also a minister in the same church—that he is in good standing, and that he is a man of moral probity and Christian character. Some of us have known him for many years as a reputable, useful, pious man. We are all personally acquainted with him, and we have no hesitancy in recommending him to personal and public confidence.

REV. GEORGE BROWN, D. D.
REV. A. H. BASSETT,
Ag't M. P. Book Concern.
REV. A. H. TRUMBO,
Assistant Ag't M. P. Book Concern.
REV. D. B. DORSEY, M. D.,
Editor *Western Methodist Protestant.*"

"OFFICE OF MILITARY COMMISSION,
Memphis, Tenn, May 11, 1863.

* * * * * "The large number of men he recruited for my regiment, and the hardships which he endured, to uphold the Flag of the Free, point out Captain Geer to the historian as a brave and true man. * * * But two days before the memorable battle of Shiloh, he was captured while making a bold and vigorous dash at the enemy, within two miles of our encampment. * * * * The tears are now filling my eyes as I look back upon that bloody battle-field, and remember the havoc and slaughter of my heroic boys of the Forty-Eighth!

"The brave men who, upon that occasion, maintained the fortunes of our bleeding country, have ever since been the subjects of persecution and calumny by those base cowards who ran from the battle-field and hid themselves in ravines and gulches at Shiloh, and the contemptible traitors whose tongues are as the tongues of serpents at home.

"Your sincere friend,

PETER J. SULLIVAN,

Colonel 48th Reg't Ohio Volunteers."

Since his return from Dixie, Captain Geer and Lieutenant William Pittenger (one of the survivors of that heroic scouting party sent into the heart of Georgia by General Mitchell), have been doing good service for the Union cause in the North by public lectures. Both are well-tried soldiers and effective speakers. Both are temporarily disabled, but expect soon to re-enter the army. Lieutenant Pittenger has prepared a volume of his experience, as a prisoner in the South, which will be a desirable companion to the book whose thrilling pages are now opened to *you*, reader. Turn forward, and read.

A. C.

BEYOND THE LINES;

OR

A YANKEE PRISONER LOOSE IN DIXIE.

CHAPTER I.

Leave Camp Dennison—Under the Enemy's Fire—Attacked in Force—A Struggle for Liberty—Captured.

On the 17th of February, 1862, the Forty-eighth Ohio regiment of volunteer infantry, under command of Colonel P. G. Sullivan, left Camp Dennison, landing at Paducah, Kentucky, and on the 4th of March, was ordered to Savannah, Tennessee. As our fleet made its way up the river, it was a sight at once grand and beautiful. It was composed of one hundred large steamers, laden to the guards with soldiers, cattle, and munitions of war. The river was at high water mark. Through its surging waters our noble vessels ploughed their way, sending forth vast volumes of smoke, which shadowed and sooted the atmosphere from hill to hill across the river valley. Over our heads waved proudly the old banner—emblem of the free. All hearts seemed anxious to meet the foe who had sought to strike down that flag, and the hopes and liberties of which it is representative.

A cry was heard on board that the enemy was near. A moment more, and he opened fire upon us, to which we very promptly replied, and with good effect, for he soon dispersed, while none of our men received injury.

Continuing our way onward we stopped at Hamburg on the 11th of March; but, owing to the great freshet, were unable to disembark, and the next day were obliged to fall back to Pittsburg, where we effected a landing on the 13th. In the mean time, I was appointed on the staff of Colonel Ralph D. Buckland, then acting as Brigadier of the Fourth Brigade, under General Sherman, who commanded the First Division. Most of us landed by the 15th, and parties were sent out every day to reconnoitre, and many returned, reporting fights with the enemy, and the capture of prisoners, horses, and other valuables.

On the 28th, we had quite a bloody conflict in a cotton-field, belonging to Mr. Beach, who was the owner of a small lot of cotton. The rebels had robbed him of all his horses, pork, and wheat, leaving him nothing but the cotton and a small amount of corn, which the Government intended to purchase. But when we were dispatched for it, we found that the rebels, who were now in full retreat, had rolled the cotton against a corn-crib, and set both on fire. The next day we had a fight near the same spot. Again, the next day, a reconnoissance showed the enemy to be in full force. On the 3d of April, the Fourth Brigade was sent out, and the skirmishers who were deployed, were soon fired upon. Col. Buckland then sent me forward to order the two companies to retreat. One of these I found was already doing so, under the command of the Major, who was in advance. The company belonging to the Seventy-second regiment stood their ground, awaiting orders.

When I rode to the top of the hill, I could see the enemy about two hundred yards distant. The lieutenant of the Seventy-second was holding his men in readiness, and just as I reached them, they arose and opened fire, at which the rebels retreated to the right, evidently intending to flank us. But this was an unfortunate movement for them, as they had not proceeded far when they encountered Major Crockett, of the Seventy-second, with two hundred men, by whom they were repulsed with heavy loss. By this time I had come up with the brigade. Buckland dispatched me immediately to order Crockett to fall back, but to continue fighting while retreating. As I proceeded on my way to Crockett—who, indeed, was a brave and daring officer—I met a lady of advanced age, in great distress. She was wringing her hands and crying:

"Oh, my son! Oh, my son! Save me and my poor son!"

I rode forward to Crockett, and found that he had repulsed the enemy, and was falling back in order.

Being alone, and in advance of the retreating companies, I again encountered the old lady on the same spot where I first saw her. Inquiring the cause of her grief, I learned that the rebels had been at her house, representing themselves as Union men, and that she had expressed herself to them, without disguise or reserve. They had thereupon seized her son, tied him on a horse, and bore him away, intending to press him into their service. My heart ached at the recital of this sad story, and at the thought of the suffering and agony to which so many families, between the two great armies, would be subjected. My sincere prayer to God, was that he would sustain the right, and send confusion amidst the foes of freedom and humanity. The old lady seemed very apprehensive they would learn that she had divulged to me the facts alluded to. Thus it is by *fear* that the loyal in heart are kept in submission. Thus, the tyrant's power rules and dominates in the South. Wherever oppression and tyranny reign, they must have for their basis, violence and brute force—and these beget fear. It is as true that fear casts out love, as it is that "love casts out fear."

We returned to camp, and that night we felt confident that our pickets were in danger. The dreary hours passed slowly away, bringing at last the light of another morning. Our pickets were then extended; and on returning from this duty, I remarked to Buckland that I believed we would be attacked before night. But he thought not, and requested me to retire to my tent, and seek repose. I went, but concluded to write to my wife. About two o'clock that afternoon, the rebels opened fire upon our pickets. I instantly mounted my horse that I had left standing at the door, and rode with all speed to the picket line, where I discovered that the rebels had captured Lieutenant Herbert and seven privates. The Seventy second, Forty-eighth, and Seventieth were soon rallied; and I thought if no fight now ensued, it would be no fault of mine, eager as I was for the fray. So I rode rapidly up the Tennessee river, in order to strike the Hamburg road, aware that I could see up that road about one mile, and thus discover what was going on.

As I was proceeding, I perceived, at a little distance, two rebels, who fled at my approach. I soon reached the road, and discovered, to my great surprise, that it was lined with rebels as far as I could see. I soon wheeled my horse, and, with accelerated speed, made my way back to General Buckland. He again dispatched me to inform Major Crockett to retreat in order.

On my way thither, these words greeted my ear:

"Halt dar! halt dar!"

I responded by firing my revolver, as a signal that I did not design to comply with the peremptory demand so euphoniously expressed. The words proceeded from two rebels, whom I discovered approaching me. They fired, and both loads took effect in my horse's shoulder. But he did not fall. Applying my spurs, he sprang down a little declivity, where the rebels stood with their empty guns. One of them struck at me with his empty weapon. I attempted to parry the blow with my left hand, and received a severe wound, having my second finger broken, which was thus rendered useless for life. The instant discharge of my revolver resulted in breaking an arm of this foe, and I immediately turned to my second antagonist, who was hastily reloading his gun. The contents of another barrel at once disabled him. This was all the work of a moment. Just at this juncture, it began to rain in torrents; and before I realized my situation, I discovered that I was surrounded by about fifty rebels. The rain and the darkness in the woods, from the overhanging storm-cloud, rendered it difficult for the rebels to distinguish their own men from ours, and they made the mistake—fortunately for me, but the reverse for them—of firing at each other. Their colonel, however, soon discovered the error, and gave the command to cease firing. There was now no possible chance for my escape, and I instantly received a blow which felled me to the earth. How long I remained insensible I could not tell. The first thing I recollect taking cognizance of, was the act of Colonel Gladden, who, dragging me out of a pool of water into which I had fallen, demanded my surrender. I seemed to lose all thought of home, wife, friends, earth, or heaven. The absorbing thought was the success of our army.

"Will you surrender?" demanded Colonel Gladden.

"I have discharged my last bullet, sir," I replied.

He commanded me to mount my horse. I refused. My captors then seized hold of me, and, throwing me across my wounded horse, made a rapid retreat. Our boys were coming at "double quick," and so impetuous was their charge towards the enemy, who was now approaching—consisting of Beauregard's advance guard of five thousand cavalry—that they began retreating in wild confusion. More than a hundred riderless horses ran dashing past me. The conflict became general and terrific, and the mighty, sweeping onset of our brave boys was only stayed by the opening of Bragg's front battery, which incessantly poured forth its shot and shell. During this interim, myself and the guards detailed to take charge of me were located in a ravine, and hence the cannon shots passed over our heads. A rifle-ball from one of our men, however, at this juncture, brought one of the guards from his horse. A rebel colonel approached him, saying, "You are too good a *man* to die so." At this moment a second ball pierced the heart of the rebel colonel, and he dropped dead.

It was here that my horse fell and died, and I felt as if a friend had gone, whose place could not be easily filled.

There was a wild and gloomy grandeur in this battle-storm raging and booming over our heads like ten thousand thunders; and my heart was tremulous with hope at one moment, and with apprehension at another, for the fate of our gallant braves. Alas! my soul mourned when I found they had been driven back by the overwhelming force of the enemy.

CHAPTER II.

First Sight of a Rebel Camp—Arraigned before Generals Jackson, Bragg, Hardee, Beauregard and Johnson—A Storm in Camp—Bayoneting a Sleeping Man (?)—Inside View of a Rebel Prison—"Calico Bill"—An Escape—Rebel Exaggerations.

In due time, I was conveyed to General Jackson. What a scene was opened to view! What a motley, mongrel, nondescript crowd did rebeldom here present! Old and young, bond and free, small and great, black and white, with countenances forlorn, agonized, or ferocious, with limbs mangled and torn. Sorrowful were the wailings of the wounded, and bitter the imprecations of the chagrined and discomfited crew.

Colonel Gladden and four privates were my escort to Jackson's tent.

"I have brought you a Yankee, General," said Colonel Gladden.

The rebel general inquired of me my rank. I declined telling him. I was then asked for papers, and upon making examination, they found with me maps of the Hamburg road, and a small rebel fortification. As soon as they made this discovery, Jackson inquired:

"Sir, what is the number of your men?"

"We have a small skirmishing party, General," I replied. "You have not captured them all to-day, and you will not to-morrow."

"Sir," he answered sharply, "you know the number, and if you do not inform me, and that promptly, I shall have you punished."

"I shall not inform you," said I, coolly; "you affirm that you are going there to-morrow, and if so, you can then see for yourself."

Somewhat enraged at this, he again threatened that he would punish me.

"Proceed with your punishment, sir," was my rejoinder; "but I shall reveal to you nothing that I think it my duty to withhold."

"I will refer you to General Bragg," said Jackson.

"Refer me to whom you please."

I was then taken before General Bragg. On our way thither, much excitement prevailed in the crowd, to many of whom the sight of a Yankee was as great a curiosity as one of Du Chaillu's famous gorillas. Various remarks saluted my ear, such as "What a big man he is." "Why! do Yankees look that thar way?"

"Why! golly, they're better looking fellows nor we are."

Such expressions are significant of that stratum of society which exists in the South to an almost incredible extent.

When we arrived at General Bragg's quarters, some men were engaged in placing in a rude box, the body of a man who had been shot by Bragg's orders, for attempting to escape to our lines. I was not without apprehensions that such would be my own fate. Still, my mind was more occupied as to what was to be the result of the battle that had just begun. The long-haired monster in human shape stood over the dead man's remains, swearing that "it was good enough for him." Just as we were entering Bragg's tent, a rough, uncouth-looking fellow, exclaimed:

"Tarnation! are you going to shoot this ere fellow?" pointing to me.

"No," said one of the guards, "we are going to keep him for a show, by golly."

I began soon to realize that the chances for my life were growing less and less. The charges arrayed against me, were for firing and killing six men, after I had been surrounded. I neither affirmed nor denied. The full results of my firing I did not know. I made up my mind, however, that whatever fate was before me, I would exhibit no shrinking or fear. It seemed probable that my doom was to be shot, and I felt impelled to answer their interrogatories in a somewhat defiant manner. The following dialogue ensued:

Bragg. "Well, sir, you are a prisoner."

Geer. "You have me in your power, sir."

B. "You have not surrendered, they say."

G. "But you have me in your possession."

B. "Well, sir, what is the number of your troops at Pittsburg Landing?"

G. "That I do not feel disposed to communicate."

B. "But we will make you communicate."

G. "You cannot do that."

B. "We will punish you, and that severely."

G. "Punish if you will, I shall not reveal to you anything I deem it proper to withhold."

B. "Well, sir, I will refer you to General Hardee, and there you will get justice. You abolitionists think you are playing h—ll over there, don't you?"

G. "We are only sending home some of her stray inmates."

B. "Be careful how you talk, sir." Turning to a rebel officer, the speaker continued: "Colonel, take this man to General Hardee, and give him all the particulars." (*Handing him a note addressed to Hardee.*)

I was thereupon placed on a stolen horse, and conducted to General Hardee.

On my way from Bragg's to Hardee's quarters, my mind was busied with singular fancies. I thought of rebel treachery and oppression; I thought of the arch-conspirators at Montgomery, the disgraceful bombardment of Sumpter, the murder of United States troops in the streets of Baltimore, the enslavement of four millions of Adam's race, all by the hateful power that now had me in its clutches. These atrocities made me the more willing to suffer in the defense of the Government that I had volunteered to serve.

Hardee is a noble-looking man, and on this occasion was dressed in full uniform of blue cloth.

"General," said my conductor, "here is a Yankee officer, referred to you by General Bragg."

"For what purpose?" asked the General.

"For examination, sir."

The General, with a look of surprise and indignation, replied:

"I shall ask the young man no questions that I would not answer myself under similar circumstances. But," added he, after a moment's consideration, "I shall send you to General Beauregard."

I could hardly repress a smile at this decision, for now, thought I, I shall see the chiefest rebel of them all.

We passed through motley crowds of long-haired "butternuts," to a place called Monterey. The General-in-Chief's headquarters were in a dilapidated cabin. I was immediately arraigned before a bony-faced old man with a gray moustache, not at all prepossessing in personal appearance. Yet, on closer observation, I could detect a cunning shrewdness and a penetrating forethought in his tones and manner.

Beauregard. "You have been rather unfortunate to-day, sir."

Geer. "Yes, sir, a little so to-day, but not so much on other days." (I referred to the four days' skirmishing prior to the Shiloh fight, in which we had seriously worsted the rebels.)

B. "Sir, they tell me you have not surrendered."

G. "No, sir; but you have me in your power."

B. "What are your reasons for not surrendering?"

G. "I decline telling you, sir."

B. "But you *shall* tell me!"

G. "If you press me, I will tell you. I surrender to no foe that can not look me in the face nationally."

When I had uttered these words, great excitement prevailed. In the din and confusion, I could discover the cry, "Cut his head off!" But in the midst of the melee, General Beauregard ordered silence, and said he would refer me to General Johnson.

As I was leaving Beauregard's quarters, I heard that gentleman say:

"We intend to go on from victory to victory, till we drive you invaders from our soil."

"Yes," replied I, for I felt his remarks keenly, "just as you did at Fort Donelson."

I left in the midst of the bitterest imprecations, escorted by a heavy guard. By this time it had grown quite dark; and as my clothing was very wet, I began to suffer with the cold.

Still conducted by the colonel, I soon came to Johnson's headquarters, which were upon the battle-field. In a tent adjoining that of Johnson, a court-martial was in session, presided over by the General, and into this tent I was taken, where the following colloquy ensued:

Col. G. "General Johnson, I have brought you a Yankee prisoner, sir."

Gen. J. "Yes, sir."

Col. G. "General, what are you going to do with him?"

Gen. J. "Treat him like a man. Bring in the surgeon and dress his wounds, and give him something to eat."

A colored boy was immediately called, and I was soon engaged in discussing the merits of a warm supper. After finishing the meal, I was taken out and seated by a fire near the tent, still closely watched and heavily guarded. I heard the General say to the court-martial that "the charges against the prisoner were, 1st. For firing after he was surrounded; 2d. For injuring our men by firing; and 3d. That he never surrendered."

"Now," said Johnson, "if he had first surrendered, and then fired and injured our men, he would have been guilty, and the court-martial might have condemned him. But inasmuch as he did *not* surrender, he is not liable to the death punishment. In regard to this third charge, I will remark that you can not legally court-martial a man for not surrendering. And now," continued he, addressing the officers, "do you know that, if I had been placed in similar circumstances, I would have done just as he did?"

It would be impossible for me to describe the emotions I then experienced. Until I heard this, I had not indulged the faintest hope of life. Johnson handed me a paper, and said:

"Will you please sign this parole that you will report at Corinth to-morrow?"

I declined to do this, for I hoped that if I could make my escape to the Union lines that night, I could impart information of great value to our army.

When I declined, the rebel Colonel said, "There, General, I told you what he was." General Johnson replied:

"Detail a guard of six men to take charge of him, and treat him well."

The guard was brought, and amidst their guns and bayonets, I was led away.

They conducted me to a tent on the hill, near a small ravine, whose waters flowed into the Tennessee. From the locality of the ground, I thought that if I could run the guards that night, I could find my way to the river, and thence back to my brigade. Lying down in the tent, which was now my prison, I awaited patiently the development of events, hoping the while that the guards might soon be blest by

"I attempted to roll quietly away from the wretch, and might have succeeded, had I not encountered a guard, who thrust me with his bayonet, exclaiming, 'Halt, dar!'"—Page 39.

the gentle embrace of slumber. I feigned sleep and snored prodigiously.

"How sound that Yankee sleeps," I heard one of the guards remark.

About midnight a storm arose, and threatened destruction to my tent, which was shortly after blown over by an auspicious blast. It instantly occurred to me that perchance there was now an opportunity to escape, in the darkness and noise of the storm. I attempted to roll quietly away from the wreck, and might have succeeded had I not encountered a guard, who thrust me with his bayonet, exclaiming, "Halt, dar!" I inquired as innocently as I could, "You wouldn't bayonet a sleeping man, would you?"

"Oh!" said he, apologetically, "I thought you was awake."

"Why! our tent has blown over, don't you see?"

The tent was soon put up, and I again safely ensconced within its canvas walls. The next day I was taken to Corinth, in a mule wagon, and deposited in a rickety old warehouse. Among the prisoners here were about twenty slaves, some of them almost white, and all clad in rags. Also in the company were ten or a dozen Tennesseeans, yclept "political prisoners," together with a few rebel soldiers.

Among the latter was a droll genius, who answered to the name of "Calico Bill," who was under sentence of death for flogging his captain. By some means he had procured an old United States uniform, in which he donned the dignity of a brigadier. In this garb he would frequently assume the position of drill-master, and the poor imbecile clay-eaters would obey his orders with the menial servitude of slaves. His conduct, while it was highly tyrannous, was nevertheless amusing. He seemed to have these ignorant soldiers completely under his control, and I refer to this illustration of slavish fear to "point the moral," if not "to adorn the tale." It does not require very profound penetration to ascertain the fact that all through the South "the schoolmaster has long been *abroad*." I have sometimes thought that if our present conflict resulted in no other good, it would send light to many a benighted spot, and, perchance,

> "Pour fresh instruction o'er the mind,
> Breathe the enlivening spirit, and fix
> The generous purpose in the glowing breast."

Not a man in the prison with us could read!

Bill practiced largely upon their credulity, and when he desired a little "contraband" fun, he would go to the window, which was always crowded outside with "secesh," and cry out:

"What will you have?"

"We want to see a Yankee," they frequently answered.

"Well, now you see *me*, and what do you think of us?"

"What are you 'uns all down here fighting we 'uns fur?

Bill would reply: "For a hundred and sixty acres of land and your negroes."

"Calico Bill" was a genuine, shrewd and intelligent Yankee, from the State of Maine. He gave me a sketch of his history, in which I learned that he was teaching in a private family in Florida, when the war broke out, was pressed into the Confederate service, and had quarreled with his captain, who undertook to exercise an authority over him, incompatible with his native freedom. He said he would rather meet his fate there than to die in the rebel army. He said there were many Northern men in their army, and that three-fourths of them would vote for the old banner and Constitution, if uninfluenced by their leaders. "But," he added, "you see how this fellow does" (referring to the man he had been drilling); "and there are thousands in their army just as ignorant as he."

When he went for a bucket of water, he would call out, "Come on, about thirty or forty of you infernal rebels, and go with me after some water!"

In this way he would drill these guards, so that those on the outside thought him a Federal, while those on the inside believed him to be a rebel officer.

In the rear of the warehouse was a counting-room; and the entire prison could boast but one bed, for which I, being the only officer, got the preference. It consisted of an old coffee-sack, filled with "body-guards," and I reluctantly accepted its use.

While standing near the door, two men came in who were dressed in Federal uniforms. They came to me and asked me if I was a Federal officer.

"No," said I, "not now; but I was a few days ago. I am a prisoner now."

In conversation with them, I ascertained that they were northern men, but, being in the South when the war broke out, were pressed, like thousands of others, into the rebel army. At the battle of Belmont, they deserted and joined the Fourth United States Cavalry, but were afterwards taken prisoners at Shiloh, and had been recognized as deserters. That day they had had their trial before General Bragg, who sentenced them to be shot on the following Tuesday. I at once became interested in their escape; and, forgetting my wounded and painful hand, and the disagreeableness of my situation, I pondered the fate of these men late into that dismal night. On the evening of the same day, a piece of file and a knife had been found upon a shelf in the prison. We converted the knife into a saw, and with this sawed off one of the planks of the floor, thereby making an aperture sufficient to permit a man to pass through. By this means, these two men, in company with "Calico Bill," made their escape. The hole I afterwards carefully concealed by placing the bed over it. We had agreed with the Tennesseeans that they should answer to the names of the escaped prisoners when the rebel officer came to the door to call the roll of the inmates of the prison. This they continued to do until Monday, at which time I was taken to Columbus, Mississippi.

We had only one meal of victuals during the forty-eight hours we remained in the prison, and there were quite a number of men there who did not get anything to eat. But for this we had some apology, in the fact that the armies were fighting very near us, and about all these rebels could do was to lie and boast about their success on the previous evening. They brought us the news that our whole army had been captured, that they had got between our forces and the river, and had taken twenty-seven thousand prisoners, and that the remainder of the army had been driven to the gunboats. So incredible and exaggerated were their reports, that when they afterward informed us of the capture of Prentiss and his division, we placed no confidence whatever in the story. On Sunday, at three o'clock, the Texan Rangers came in greatly decimated, themselves declaring that they had been cut to pieces by our sharpshooters.

CHAPTER III.

Taken to Columbus, Mississippi—Visit from the Clergy—An Enthusiastic Mute—American Aristocracy—Secession Lies—Political and Ecclesiastical Prisoners—Reflections.

ON Monday morning, at ten o'clock, a part of the prisoners left Corinth, for Columbus, Mississippi. Wherever the cars stopped, the wildest excitement prevailed.

"How goes the day?" was the constant inquiry.

We were exhibited as some of the trophies of the battle. That the people were somewhat divided, could easily be perceived from their countenances. On the evening of the same day, we arrived at Columbus, and there we were placed under a heavy guard, in an old warehouse; but the ex-Governor of Mississippi came to the prison, and took us to the hotel, where we enjoyed supper at his expense. There the crowd gathered round us as though we were some mammoth traveling menagerie, while our hostess kept commenting so earnestly upon our handsome appearance, that, in spite of my longitudinal neck and limbs, I began to suspect myself worthy the compliment. While under guard here, I heard men declaring most unequivocally their opposition to a Republican form of government. Two ministers who visited me—Rev. Doctor Tensley, of the First Baptist Church, and Rev. Mr. Morris, of the M. E. Church South—expressed but little confidence in the Confederate cause. These gentlemen invited me to their church on Sabbath, but the force of circumstances compelled me to decline the invitation. These circumstances were, close confinement under a heavy guard; and of this fact they were perfectly aware. I was led from this to believe that their sympathy was not genuine.

After the ministers left me, a deaf and dumb man came to the door, and handed me a paper which contained an article relative to the recent battle of Shiloh. The account began in the following self-gratulatory style: "Glory! glory! glory! Victory! victory! I write from Yankee paper." The writer proceeded in his intense and heated manner by saying, "Of all the victories that have ever been on record, ours is the most complete. Their repulse at Bull Run was nothing to compare to our victory at Shiloh. General Buell is killed, and General Grant wounded and taken prisoner. Soon we will prove too much for them, and they will be compelled to let us alone. Our brave boys have driven them to the river, and compelled them to flee to their gunboats. The day is ours."

The mute who had given me the paper was so permeated with the prospect of rebel success, that he favored hoisting the black flag, and in this was sustained by a large number in that neighborhood. As the news came slowly in, the comments made on the state of affairs were as various as they were amusing. Only through the friendship and ingenuity of the slaves, who were the *attaches* of the prison, were we privileged to receive papers giving the account of the recent fight. When they learned the true condition of their army after the battle, and realized that their boasted victory was a bloody defeat, they became more charitable in their opinions. I became well satisfied from the conversation I overheard from rebel officers and visitors, during my incarceration here, that a favorite doctrine of Dixie is to adjust their "peculiar institution" in such a way as to include the poor whites as well as the colored people as chattel property.

I was here visited by two rebel captains belonging to Bushrod Johnston's staff, one of whom was a lawyer from Virginia, named McMoore. These men conversed freely on the times. Both of them expressed themselves as decidedly in favor of an American Aristocracy! They argued, with as much earnestness and ability as their vocabulary furnished words, the imbecility of Republican government; and to prove the immutability of their opinions, cited to me the semi-idiotic and degraded "clay-eaters" of the South, saying:

"What do these men know of civil institutions, and what right have they to vote?"

Said I, "Gentlemen, is it possible that this is the faith of your leaders?"

They replied emphatically in the affirmative.

"Then, sirs, we of the North have not been mistaken on a subject which has been forcing itself upon us as a fact, but which we were loth to believe could harbor itself even in the basest American heart. Since you are frank enough to own it, certainly the world should know it, and execrate it as it deserves."

When I became acquainted with the motives of these two representative men—how they despised their poor, ignorant soldier-brethren, armed and fighting to fasten fetters on themselves and children for ever, I could but exclaim, "Send out thy light and thy truth, O God! into all the earth. Hasten the day when ignorance and oppression shall vanish before the free gospel, and righteousness through all the land prevail."

From my prison windows I now had ample leisure to study the countenances of all classes of our rebellious enemies, from Brigadier Generals down to the conscript "Sand-hillers." All faces were indicative of sadness. From what I could see and overhear—the downcast eyes and the conflicting stories—I was well satisfied that they had been worsted at Shiloh. The officers were given to wholesale exaggeration, their falsifying tongues gliding from lie to lie with the alacrity of a Baron Munchausen! These prevarications forcibly reminded me of a negro boy down South, who undertook to describe to his master a storm.

"Why, massa, dare was de wonderfullest, de tremendus'est post mowerfulest win' stohm dat you ever heah. De win' blowed so hard dat it blowd de har—*de har*—all off one man's head! Ya'as, de har all off one man's head! De har!"

"Now, Sam, you lying rascal, why did'nt the wind blow *your* hair off?"

"Why—why—you'se allers bodderin white folks when dey'se tellin' de trufe—why, *dare was a man a-stan'in' a-holdin my har on!* Ya'as—a man a stan'in'—a man!"

"But why was'nt his hair blown off?"

"O dare was anudder man a-standin' a-holdin' his har on! Ya'as anudder man."

"But why was'nt *his* hair blown off?"

"Kase — why — w-why, — (you'se bodderen you'sef about de wind-stohm)—why *dare was a little boy a-standin a-holdin his har on. Ya'as, a-ha*-a little boy—a holden his har on!"

"But why wasn't the little boy's hair blown off, you black scamp?"

"Why—w-why—golly, does'nt you see plain 'nuff how it was? Why, DARE WAS A MAN WID A BALD HEAD A-STANDIN' A-HOLDIN' HIS HAR ON!"

Just so the secession leaders falsify, and thus they attempt to bolster up their improbable Confederacy. The whole compact is a libelous league with darkness!

Some of these pompous Southerners would treat us with a kind of counterfeit courtesy, which became to us even more disgusting than outright abuse. The rebel army is made up of a passive-minded, illiterate citizenship, officered by slave-owners and negro-drivers. The maximum of soldiers in a regiment is much smaller than in the Federal army, and each company has three Lieutenants. This gives the young men of aristocratic families an opportunity to wear shoulder-straps and lord it over the "poor white trash," which compose the rank and file.

I learned from the prison guards, many of whom would be loyal to the old Stars and Stripes if they dared, that the mass of the Southern armies have been forced by the most stringent and often cruel measures to take up arms against the United States Government.

At this place there were a number of political prisoners, and a few prisoners of war. Once we obtained leave to visit them. We were conducted by a vigilant guard to their apartments in an upper room of a very dilapidated building. We found about one hundred and fifty Mississippi citizens, such as were suspected of Union sentiments, in a most loathsome situation. Among them were three clergymen—one a Presbyterian, one a "United Brother," and the other a Methodist. There was also a lawyer from Kentucky, named Halleck, who had been captured by Bishop General Polk. Halleck was a subject of the ecclesiastical body over which the Bishop ruled; but his loyalty to church did not save him from arrest and trouble for want of confidence in arch-treason. He had been dragged from his bed by a band of ruffians who tied his hands behind him, and forced him into a filthy prison where he lay for seven months in close confinement. He was finally permitted to share a room with thirty-five or forty other

Unionists. At one time they were so shamefully neglected, that for three days they were unsupplied with any food. To prevent absolute starvation, they were obliged to beg the guards to assist them in stealing a barrel of soap-grease, which they devoured with a greedy relish! This was in the midst of the boasted chivalry of Columbus, Mississippi!

I should not forget to mention here the names of the ex-Governor of the State, Mr. Whitefield, and his son. They had human hearts, and extended to us some degree of kindness and sympathy. But these friendships were rare exceptions, and all sufficient, if reported to rebel officials, to call down vengeance on their heads. The people, to avoid suspicion and imprisonment, were compelled to practice all manner of apparent cruelties. In this building we began to feel the hateful oppressor's power. We could hardly believe that any portion of our once united and happy country could be so soon, so darkly blighted by accursed treason!

While looking on the old, rusty walls of my prison-house, mocked and insulted by the jeering outside multitudes, I had time and heart for reflection. I thought of a familiar cottage amid the hills of Ohio, at that very hour all fair and free in the spring sunlight, the orchard blossoms, the opening flowers in garden and arbor, the dewy meadow grass, and the thousand charming scenes of my home! I thought of wife and children there—how they would wonder and fear at receiving no tidings from the one they loved. I thought of God and his cause—my country and her honor—my flag and her insulted glory. I thought of the poor Southern conscript, and the despised and fettered slave of the cotton-field, and my soul was stirred with mingled hope and compassion. Thinking of my home, my friends, my country, my wounds, my prison, I could but say:

"Patience, my soul, the Saviour's feet were worn;
The Saviour's heart and hands were weary too;
His garments stained, and travel-worn, and old,
His vision blinded with a pitying dew.
Love thou the path of sorrow that he trod,
Toil on, and wait in patience for thy rest;
Oh! country that I love, we soon shall see
Thy glorious cause triumphant, crowned and blest."

While reflecting upon the inconsistency of secession, and witnessing the persecutions heaped upon those who were loyal to the flag and truth of our fathers, I almost faltered in my religious faith, for many of these leaders in treason were professed Christians. But, through the power of prayer, came a satisfying answer to my questioning fear. I felt that the Lord Omnipotent was just—that his grace and gospel were for the poor and the oppressed.

I remembered the day when the Saviour appeared to me—when denser, darker prison-bands were sundered. Then old things passed away. Then came the strength to believe and trust in a Higher Power—an Infinite Deliverer. Remembering when the friendly voice had spoken to my troubled heart, "Peace, be still," even in prison, and hated of men for Christ's and country's sake, I could exclaim:

"Faith of our fathers, living still,
In spite of dungeon, fire, and sword;
Oh! how our hearts beat high with joy
Where'er we hear that glorious word!
Faith of our fathers! holy faith!
We will be true to thee till death!"

Though a prisoner of war, a soldier can be a Christian. He realizes in trial and trouble that the Judge of all the earth does right.

CHAPTER IV.

The Wounded from Shiloh—Inquisitive Negroes—An Abomination—A Striking Contrast—Tom—Attempted Escape—An Ingenious Darkey—Rebel Fare—The Irish Sergeant—Narrow Escape—Mending Clothes and Getting News—Horrible Scenes in Prison—A Discussion.

During my imprisonment, many wounded soldiers from Corinth, were brought to Columbus. The leading men were painfully struck at the loss of General Albert Sidney Johnson. My prison-life was romantic and instructive, and I endeavored to make a partial atonement for its deprivations. The negroes, whose business it was to bring our victuals, and keep the prison in some sort of order, were generally inquisitive in their looks, and often in their words. They wondered why so many white men were confined and guarded. I was much interested with two negro waiters, who came daily to our room, one about twelve, and the other about fifteen years of age. Said George, the younger:

"Massa, when's you gwine to take Memphis?"

"Why? George!" said one of our party.

"Kase my mother's dar, and she'll be free when de Linkum sogers gits Memphis."

"George," said I, "what do you know about freedom?"

"Why, Lor' massa, I know'd if you'd whip 'em up dar, us colored folks 'ud all be free, an' dat's what makes dem rebels fight like de debel. God bless you massa, I knows why. When de war broke out, I was livin' up in old Kentuck, and dey say now we'se got to take dis here nigger off, or else de Yankees will hab him. I hoped and prayed dat de Yankees *would* git me. God bless you, massa, *I knows*."

From this time I began to be more than ever interested in the negroes. I discovered a latent talent in the despised race. I resolved to investigate this new field of inquiry. The older one of these waiters and myself, had afterward many a friendly interview. He told me that he had been reared in New Orleans. His father was a white man, who often comforted his innocent victim, by saying that her offspring should be sent North to freedom. But when hostilities began, he entered the army, forgetful alike of his promises and his crimes. This outraged woman was afterward hired to a planter, to work in a cotton-field, while her son was sent to Columbus, as a hotel waiter. Such, thought I, are some of the barbarities of this horrid system of enslavement.

About this time a Colonel was appointed as commandant of this post, *vice* ex-Governor Whitefield. Our boarding and location were now changed, and we were placed in a back room and fed on scanty rations of corn-bread *minus* salt, and an indifferent supply of tainted meat, which emitted a very disagreeable effluvia.

While in this condition, and lying on the bare floor, a citizen entered and informed us that his brother-in-law was then a prisoner in Columbus, Ohio. He said he had been taken at Fort Donelson, and that his wife had that day received a letter from him, and that he was walking the streets of Columbus, carrying his side-arms, and boarding at the American House!

This statement aroused my indignation. I never before felt so keenly my condition, and when he attributed the lenity of our government to cowardice and a disposition to admit the superiority of southern claims and dignity, and stigmatized us as "invaders" of their soil and suffering justly as such, I could not restrain the fiery wrath that burned within me. I have a faint recollection of seeing the man hurrying in greedy haste from the prison, doubtless impelled by the fear of something to come.

Again we were indebted to the kind services of our ever-faithful and unwavering friends of the race despised. One, who flourished under the sobriquet of "Tom," rendered us efficient aid. Our object was to escape from the prison, and for this purpose Tom brought us a rope and chisel. With the chisel, I cut a hole through the prison floor, but after laboring faithfully for some time, I discovered that the room below was filled to the ceiling with boxes and bales containing commissary stores. I had arranged with Tom, who had brought me a desiderated map of Mississippi and Tennessee, to leave that night, he occupying a station on the outside, ready to aid me if necessary, and supplied with sufficient provisions for my contemplated flight.

When I found myself foiled in my effort to pass through the floor, I turned my attention to the hearth of the room, which I took up, intending to let myself down at that point, and make my escape through a window below, which was covered by a projecting roof. But just as I was about to take away the key-stone of the hearth, I heard the guard cry out, "*Corporal o' de guard, post number fo',*" which arrested my attention, and moving toward the window, discovered in the darkness of the night, that the rain was falling in torrents. Again my ear caught the voice of the guard, who, in his peculiar Southern intonations, was addressing the corporal.

"I's gittin' all wet; put me undah dat ar windah, dar."

So the guard was stationed under the window where I had contemplated making my exit, and all my plans, for the nonce, were frustrated.

Early the next morning Tom came to the door and said:

"*Why* you don' didn't come, massa?"

"Why, Tom, that room below is full of commissary stores."

"Why, massa, I don' ought to have told you dat, but I don' didn't know it."

Tom came in, and I exhibited the hole in the floor, and assured him that if the fact of its existence were not concealed, I should be either sent to jail or hung. He looked at it, and fruitful as he was of expedients, soon devised a remedy. He first tacked a piece of carpet over the hole, and afterward, finding that it would yield if trodden upon, constructed a rude seat immediately above it.

This, and other manifestations of intellectual and mechanical aptness, led me into a train of reflection concerning a race so decried and degraded. I asked with Campbell—

"Was man ordained the slave of man to toil,
Yoked with the brutes, and fettered to the soil;
Weighed in a tyrant's balance with his gold?
No! Nature stamped us in a heavenly mould!
She bade no wretch his thankless labor urge,
Nor, trembling, take the pittance and the scourge."

From this time I became deeply interested in my African protege. He seemed keenly alive to his condition. He told me in a conversation that "the colored people were all heathens—they knew nothing. I was talking," he added, "with massa and missus dis mornin', and missus asked me, 'Tom what you tink of dem Yankees?'

"'Ah,' says I, 'missus, I don' don't like em at all. Dey won't have nothin' to say to a nigger.' Den missus said, ses she.

"'Tom, don't you know dese Yankees are comin' down har to confisticate all you cullod people?' Now, she tink I don' don't know what 'confisticate' means; spec' she tinks I tought it was *to kill.* God bless you, massa, I knows it is to *free de darkies*, and den dis pore nigger have hoss and carriage, if I don' can work and pay for 'em. While I was talkin' wid massa and missus, I stood and shake all over. I tells 'em dat I is so 'feared dat dey would come dat I don't know what for to do. God bless you, don't you tink dey was fool enough to tink I *was* afeerd. Ha! ha! ha!"

The hours wore heavily on in that dreary prison-house. Tom brought our food in an old trough, which had doubtless been employed in feeding swine, and we were compelled to take in food in genuine primitive style. In a short time, we received intelligence that we were to be removed to another apartment in the same building, and I began to feel a degree of uneasiness lest my effort to escape should be discovered by the hole in the floor. Tom again befriended me. He ascertained that a printing-press was to be put up in the room the prisoners had occupied, and while assisting in the work succeeded in placing a portion of the stationary materials in such a manner as to effectually secrete the aperture.

As I have already intimated, our supply of food grew "smaller by degrees and horribly less." Our gastronomic propensities were however, occasionally regaled by some delicacies (?) smuggled to us by Tom and his brother Pete. We did not care then to inquire whether they obtained them honestly or not, but the probability is that they were appropriated from their master's larder.

One of our chief annoyances in this prison was in the person of a diminutive, pompous, and arrogant Irishman named Mackey, who seemed to rejoice in the title of "sergeant," which he took great care to frequently ventilate in the presence of the prisoners. He was an orderly of the provost-marshal, and the fellow, clothed with a little brief authority, seemed to be impressed with the sole idea that tyranny was the only attribute of one so exalted. Once, when he came into my quarters, I asked him what object he could have in the rebel army, and what profit he expected to derive from the establishment of a confederacy?

"Enough, be jabers," he replied. "You Yankees want to free our nagers, be sure, and we're all ferninst that here, and we won't submit at all, at all."

"How many negroes have *you*, Mr. Mackey," I asked.

"Why, sure, and be jabers, and I haven't a nager in the world."

"Well, sir, what interest then can you have in this war?"

"Och, and be sure, a poor tool of an Irishman can hardly git a wee jab of work now, and if these divels were free, we'd have to go beggin' foriver."

So, selfishness, in the guise of slavery and pride, forms the substratum of the so-called Southern Confederacy.

On further conversation with the sergeant, I learned that he had really no interest in the cause of the South, that he was not in the army from choice, but as a means of obtaining a livelihood, and that he bitterly cursed rebellion in his heart as the prolific parent of untold evils.

Our new room fronted the hotel, and from some of the officers we obtained permission to stand upon the balcony of the prison during a part of each evening. On one occasion we were ordered back by the guards. I hesitated a moment; but in that moment a guard leveled his piece and drew the trigger. Fortunately for me the gun missed fire, but at the same moment another guard fired, and killed a deaf man who had thrust his head from an upper window. Realizing the danger to which I was exposed, I instantly withdrew.

On the same evening, I noticed an unusual excitement among the rebel officials. To ascertain its cause I again had recourse to Tom. He requested me to tear a hole in my coat, and then order him, in the presence of the guards, to take it to some tailor for repairs. He insisted that I should speak angrily to him, for such a course would more effectually deceive the guards. I did as he had directed, and he demurred, declaring that he wished dem "Yankees would mend dar own close." The guards in a peremptory tone commanded him to get the coat, and have it repaired forthwith. This was what Tom desired; and with many protestations of hatred toward the whole Yankee race, he, with great apparent reluctance, carried the garment from the prison.

In a short time he returned, seemingly in the same mood, and with well-feigned indignation, handed over the coat. On examination I found a newspaper in one of the pockets which contained an account of the evacuation of Corinth, the surrender of Island No. 10, and the bombardment of Fort Pillow, New Orleans, and other important information of which we had previously known nothing! This little artifice and its successful management, while it furnished me with very cheering intelligence, also gave me an elevated opinion of Tom's native talents.

Other prisoners continued to arrive, many of whom had been wounded in the battle of

Shiloh, and new quarters were prepared for them. They were incarcerated in an old stone building not far from our prison, and although wounded and almost famished, were compelled to lie upon the hard floor, their wounds undressed, and their physical wants unattended to. I obtained permission to visit them, and as I entered the house my eyes were pained by a sight that beggars description. Eighteen prisoners, "crushed by pain and smart," occupied the room. There were men in that room who had been wounded for two weeks, and who, during that whole time, had not received the slightest attention. The result had been that their wounds were tainted with putrid flesh, and alive with crawling maggots! I obtained a list of their names at the time, but, as the reader will hereafter learn, was subsequently compelled to burn it. The only apology the rebel authorities could offer for this brutal neglect was that they were too busily employed in attending to the wants of their own to look to the welfare of others.

Many of the men died, some from their wounds, and others from disease. The sad and sickening scenes of prison life daily harrowed up the soul's keener susceptibilities, and one by one they yielded up their lives a sacrifice for liberty.

On one occasion, I heard the guards engaged in an animated discussion concerning their participation in the war. One of them remarked:

"Bill, you and I are both poor men, and what in the name of God are we fighting for?"

"Why, Tom, you haven't turned traitor to the Confederacy, have you?"

"No," said he, "I can't say that I have, but I'd like mighty well to know what profit this whole thing will be to us poor people. I have a family, you know; and I have been forced to leave them, and here I am. You know how everything hes riz. There's flour now, and you can't git a barrel for less nor forty dollars, and pork is fifty dollars a hundred, and there aint a bit of salt to be got for love nor money. Now, I'd jist like to know what a man's family is going to do under such circumstances?"

Bill answered by saying:

"This war aint a-going to last long. How'll them fellers do without cotton. They'll have to give in afore two months, for all their manufactures have stopped now."

"Don't you believe a word of that 'ere stuff. It's all gammon, I tell you. They can do without *us* a great deal better nor we can do without *them.* They've got the whole world to resort to, and can git their supplies anywhere they please."

"Yes, I know that; but then they haint got anything other nations want. It was *our* cotton what brought all the gold and silver into the country."

"There's that old song again. Why, they've got the best perducing land in the world. And their corn and cattle aint to be sneezed at the world over."

"Well, that may all be true," rejoined the other, "but they can't whip us."

"Well, suppose we whip them, what will be gained?"

"Why, we'll stop the 'tarnal thieves from stealing our niggers."

"Now that's a grand mistake. Don't you see every nigger in the South will break right for the North, for there won't be no Fugitive Slave Law then. And then you know what a dreadful time we had not long ago up Lowndes county with the niggers, for this here country's got twice as many niggers as whites."

At this an angry dispute arose between them, one declaring the other an abominable Yankee, and the other as stoutly denying it. Oaths were freely bandied, and the loyal Southerner threatened to call the corporal of the guard, and have the other arrested. The latter in the mean time continued to protest that he had said nothing detrimental to Southern interests.

"Well, how did you know," said the rabid secessionist, "about the cattle and corn in New York, if you had never lived there?"

"But I have been there, though I never lived in that region."

"Well, if that's the case," responded his antagonist, "you had better keep mighty quiet about it, or we'll treat you like we did John Peterson, that miserable Yankee that we hung last week to a pine tree."

Just then the relief-guard came, and the conversation ceased. I noted down at the time the dialogue as it occurred, gave the manuscript subsequently to my friend Captain Steadman, who, in connection with other papers, as the reader will presently learn, carried it to Washington city, where I received it from him.

From all this, which was spoken in a most angry and boisterous manner, and while I held my ear to the key-hole of the prison-door, I learned what excessive antipathy the Southern people, as a mass, entertain towards persons of Northern birth. As the reader follows me through this book, other evidences of Southern ignorance, malice, and inhumanity will arise, all of which I witnessed or experienced, and all of which are related with no spirit of hatred, but as an "ower true tale." I do not relate these facts in the spirit of a politician, nor for political purposes; for the nativity, education, and political antecedents of myself and of the entire family from which I sprung, have developed a warm support of Democratic principles. To these I yet ardently adhere, though positively and absolutely repudiating that form thereof which in the slightest degree affiliates with treason or oppression.

CHAPTER V.

Southern Inhumanity—A Prison Telegraph—Mobile—Conversation with a Fire-Eater—Negro Sale Stables—A Bad Sign—Mule Beef—Montgomery—In the Penitentiary—Felon Soldiers—Hanging for Theft—Visit to a Condemned Prisoner—Who Shall Answer?

OUR condition now became so painful and distressing, that, as a last resort, we determined to petition the authorities for a redress of our grievances. We had neither beds nor blankets, and the allowance of rations doled out to us was insufficient to sustain life. A lieutenant in the Confederate service, a poor, illiterate fellow, not possessed of education sufficient to call the muster-roll correctly, entered the prison and threatened to place Major Crockett—of whom we have spoken before—in irons, simply because he had referred, in the Lieutenant's presence, in no very favorable terms, to the character of our treatment. We had made application personally to Colonel McClain, then commandant of the post, and who, we learned, was a professed Christian. We were careful to appeal to his Christianity as a means of awakening an interest in our behalf. His reply was as follows:

"You invaders! you abolitionists! you that

are *stealing* our property! *you* talk about Christianity! You should be the last men to utter a word on that subject."

A lieutenant in our ranks, named Herbert, answered him by saying:

"If your so-called Southern Confederacy cannot furnish us with enough to eat, just inform us and we will acquaint our government of the fact."

This seemed to irritate the doughty Colonel, and he replied very fiercely:

"I'll let you know that we have a government strong enough to hold *you*. You will have to go into close confinement."

In a short time four men with loaded guns entered, and took Lieutenant Herbert from the prison. What was to be his fate we knew not, but in five days he returned, his appearance indicating that he had been exposed to severe treatment. He told me that he was taken to the old county jail, was there incarcerated in a damp, filthy, and bedless cell, swarming with odious vermin, and from which a negro had recently been taken to be executed. This barbarous outrage was inflicted for the sole purpose, in the language of his tormentor, "of letting him know that there was a Southern Confederacy."

The sick and wounded prisoners in the room above us were suffering intensely, and we were not allowed the privilege of visiting them. In order to hold any communication at all with the inmates above, we were compelled to resort to an expedient which answered our purpose for the time. We obtained a small wire, and by letting it down from the upper window to the one below, and attaching a written communication to it, opened up a kind of telegraphic connection between the two departments of the prison. In this way we were daily informed of the transactions of our friends above.

We were now about to leave the prison, and we quitted it, feeling with Bishop King, that

> "A prison is in all things like a grave,
> Where we no better privileges have
> Than dead men; nor so good."

We were next taken to Mobile, Alabama. On our way thither, I conversed with a number of Southrons, among whom was an insignificant personage from South Carolina. He complained because their officers were not allowed to have their servants with them. He called it one of the most inhuman deprivations imaginable!

"Sir," said I, "we have been treated like

beasts and half-starved here on your southern soil; what do you think of that?"

"O," he replied, "that's all right enough for you 'uns; but *we* belong to the first families of South Carolina!"

"Your logic is vain, sir, for we of the free North recognize no officer in the army as made of better stuff than the least drummer-boy in the service. Your 'first families' were the prime movers in this rebellion, being the degenerate descendants of bankrupt royalists and luckless adventurers." The truth cut him severely, and he began to curse the "mudsills" of the North, ridiculing that pure democracy which lifts up the poor and levels down the rich. When I referred to our free schools and our general information as a people, he raved like a madman. His ignorance boiled over in froth and fury, only to emphasize the corrupting effects of the bastard aristocracy of the South.

We arrived in Mobile on Sabbath morning, the 26th of May. Here, too, we could detect an undercurrent of Union sentiment in the humane treatment we received. I knew full well, however, the odium in which the Mobilians held all who opposed human bondage as legalized in the Confederacy. I felt that we were indeed among enemies and barbarians. We were driven like yoked bondmen to the heart of the city, and there halted in the crowded streets for about two hours and a half beneath a sweltering Alabama sun, after which we were thrust into the negro sale stables. Of course we were fatigued and sickened by such outrageous treatment, but we bore it all as patiently as grace would allow. As we entered these human chattel stalls where many poor hearts had sorrowed before, we noticed this inscription over our stable door.

"NEGROES FOR SAIL AND GOOD FEALD HANDS."

During our stay in this place there was quite a stir among the rebels. The astounding fact was revealed that the mules slain at Shiloh had been barreled up and forwarded to Mobile to feed Yankee prisoners! When this abomination was made known to the commandant, he immediately ordered the mule-beef to be thrown into the river; and in order to redeem his government from the merited contempt of the civilized world, he published the facts in the Mobile papers. A copy of a daily paper containing the information was furnished us by a negro, and we had the satisfaction of reading the history of our rations!

The commandant's motives in publishing this

barbarity were not appreciated by the chivalrous (?) authorities, and he was himself arrested and imprisoned for an act that even cannibals might blush to condemn.

The negroes, who were shrewder and more manly than their masters, were our faithful friends and news-bearers. They all understood how to furnish us papers in the manner described in a previous chapter. The results of the mule-beef investigation plainly proved that the whole transaction was sanctioned by the Government. It was not an individual speculation by an unprincipled army contractor, but an official outrage, perpetrated by the chivalrous Confederacy!

From Mobile we were taken to Selma, from thence to Tuscaloosa, and from thence to Montgomery. Here we were placed in the penitentiary over night, until arrangements could be made for our accommodation in the military prison. Here we shared the fare of criminals, which proved to be the best I ever received in Dixie. As to the truthfulness of the report that the Confederacy had liberated their felons as soldiers, I am not prepared to speak. But while I was in the Montgomery penitentiary, during the brief space of thirty hours, two inmates were released and paid eight hundred dollars each to enter the service as substitutes. This I witnessed. The keeper of the prison informed me, on inquiring the nature of their crimes, that they were murderers. From reliable sources I learned that many criminals, from different southern prisons, were received into the army as soldiers. The two I saw were desperate-looking men.

While here I was deeply impressed at seeing a negro in an adjoining cell under condemnation of death. In order to frighten him to make such confessions as his accusers desired, the rope with which he was to be suspended from the gallows, was put in the cell with the culprit. I asked the keeper the nature of the man's offence, and was told that he was sentenced to die for stealing a watch.

"What! are you going to hang a man for stealing a watch?"

"O, yes," said my informant, "we must be severe with these niggers, or we couldn't live for them."

"But he is a valuable-looking piece of property."

"True, sir, but the State is obligated to pay one-half his value to the master, and he was appraised at sixteen hundred dollars,—so you see only one-half the loss will fall upon his master."

All this was spoken with that serious business air which showed a real sympathy with the slaveholder who was about to suffer the loss of eight hundred dollars!

On account of my crippled hand and general debility, I was privileged to walk about the hall. There I could see the doomed man who was so soon to suffer the ignominious death of the scaffold. The keeper's sympathy was altogether with the owner of the negro; but he congratulated himself in the master's behalf by saying that, since the beginning of the war, negroes were poor sale, and that for the owner of this condemned one to get half his appraised value would be very consoling in the hour of trouble! One circumstance in connection with this incident gladdened my heart. On one occasion I overheard two men conversing with the negro in his cell. They were godly men, and had come to offer the sympathy of supplication in prayer. One of these visitors was gifted in a special manner. His pleadings before the court of heaven in behalf of his unfortunate fellow-man, were touchingly eloquent. He sang and prayed alternately, and with tearful eyes and tender tones, pointed the criminal to the Saviour who blessed the dying thief on Calvary. But all his instructions and persuasions seemed alike in vain. The stoic prisoner remained hard-hearted and unmoved.

I asked and obtained permission from the keeper to speak a few words to the man so soon to die. The conditions on which I obtained the favor were that my instructions should be given in the keeper's presence.

Looking through the iron bars at my sinful but unfortunate auditor, I said,

"Do you believe that Christ died for all?"

"I don't know, massa," he replied.

"Well, you know something about the Bible, don't you?"

"No, massa."

"Have you never heard the Gospel preached?"

"Yes, massa, I used to hear old parson Cooper preach, and I guess dat was what he preached about."

"Can you read?"

"No, massa."

"Did you ever pray?"

"No, massa. I'se heard folks a-prayin'. My massa never prayed like dis nigga,"—referring to the visitor who had been praying with him in the cell.

"Well, my dear fellow, you know you have to die, don't you?"

"Yes, massa."

"What do you think will become of you when you die?"

"I dun know, massa."

"Did you ever talk with white people on this subject?"

"No, massa."

Here our conversation was interrupted by the keeper, who told me I must return to my cell. I had no further opportunity to converse with the poor negro prisoner. My thoughts troubled me. I reflected on the destiny of these immortal beings, thus oppressed in body and soul by their tyrant masters. What a fearful weight of responsibility rests *somewhere!* Who shall give account in the great day for the ignorance of the four millions of slaves, going up to judgment from a land of boasted light and knowledge? This slave was a representative man. Although he knew little about secular matters, he had opportunity to learn even less of religion!

But despite all the efforts to keep the slaves in ignorance, both by legal enactments and tyrannical vigilance, very many of them gained a surprising fund of information. What an accursed system of wrong is that which locks the Bible from the homes and hearts of the poor! May the uttermost overthrow come upon an institution that prohibits the education of any class or color of God's children!

The next day, before leaving the prison, I asked permission to visit the colored convict once more, but the privilege was not granted. That very day a dark man was hung, and a darker crime registered in the book of Judgment-day accounts, the penalty of which will by-and-by rest upon the head of the guilty perpetrators.

CHAPTER VI.

A New Prison—Murder of Lieutenant Bliss—In Irons—Yankee Ingenuity—Rebel Ignorance—Parson Rogers—Faithful Servants—Bold and Successful Escape of Prisoners—Captain Troy—A Blindfold Journey—A Traitor.

WE were now conducted to our new quarters in the military prison, a description of which I will attempt. The side walls were of brick, twenty inches in thickness, and thirteen feet high. The ends were closed by massive iron-clad wooden gates, extending the whole width of the prison. The room was about two hundred feet long, and forty in width. It was used formerly as a cotton depot. There was on either side a narrow shed-roof, sloping inward, extending two-thirds of the entire length of the building. Beneath this shelter were six hundred soldiers, and about one hundred and fifty political prisoners.

Near this prison, Lieutenant Bliss, of Illinois, one of the noblest and truest men I ever knew. and a minister of the gospel, was murdered. The circumstances of this cruel outrage are as follows: One beautiful morning in May, the Lieutenant, being somewhat indisposed, and desiring to breathe the fresh and fragrant air without our prison walls, asked permission of the Captain of the Guard, to go to an adjacent house and get his canteen filled with fresh milk. With considerable reluctance the privilege was granted, and the Lieutenant and myself were allowed to go on our errand, under a guard of four armed men. Upon our arrival at the house, Bliss handed his canteen through the window, where a lady received it, and in accordance with his request, filled it with milk, and passed it back to him. At this moment, one of the guards muttered some undistinguishable order, which I was unable to understand, although I was nearer the guard than Bliss. The command, whatever it was, of course could not be obeyed; but the guard instantly raised his gun. Bliss saw it, and remarked pleasantly, though a little excited:

"You are not going to shoot me, are you?"

No sooner were his words uttered, than the gun was fired and the bullet pierced the heart of my gallant comrade. His last words were, "Brother, I'm shot!" I stood amazed and dumb with indignation over the bleeding corpse of my faithful companion, the three remaining loaded guns pointed at me. From this scene of murder I was forced back to the prison. I felt it my duty to report this inhuman act to the commandant, and ask redress, by having the reckless guard punished. What was my astonishment and indignation to learn, afterward, that that very guard, for that very act, was granted thirty days' furlough as a reward. The only apology offered was, that possibly the guard misunderstood his instructions! I ventured to tell the commandant, Captain Troy, my opinion of such conduct, and to his face called the outrage by its proper name, a bloody murder, committed under his guilty authority. As I might have expected, this plain language brought down his vengeful wrath, and he replied:

"I will put you in irons, sir."

I could but reply, thinking of my dear, lost comrade:

"I am in your power, sir, irons or no irons; but you murdered my sick friend, and are guilty of shedding his blood!"

For my impertinence, I was handcuffed and made to suffer the cruel spite of my hateful enemies.

These things occured in the city of Montgomery, Alabama, among the chivalry of the South.

We often suffered for water in this cotton-shed prison. Some of our boys resolved to dig a well within the walls. In digging, they came to a stratum of potters' clay, by which, after the well was completed, they passed many a leisure hour in manufacturing little wares, such as pipes, rings, cups, &c., all of which found a ready sale among the rebels, and commanded a fair price in Confederate shinplasters. The ingenuity of our Yankee boys was a constant marvel to the stupid Southrons. We received sufficient pocket money by our manufactures to furnish us with many little conveniences and comforts. One of our comrades, who had formerly been an engraver, and who had no conscientious scruples about using the rebel currency to the best advantage, was very skilful in changing five cent scrip to fifties, and many of the fives that were *passed in* for our wares, *passed out* fifties for gingerbread!

One day quite a commotion prevailed among the rebel peddlers in our prison. A gaunt, gawking fellow had received one of these changed bills, but was not quite satisfied of its genuineness. A motley crowd were huddled around him trying to unravel the mystery. I was called by the holder of the bill to explain. Said the puzzled critic, holding out the suspected paper and pointing to the redundant cipher at the right of the five:

"Look here, Capt'n, at this tarnal round thing here. This thing ortn't fur to be here."

"Well, sir," said I, "I can't help it; why did you put it there?"

"I didn't put it thar, nuther. I got it uv that thar feller," said he, pointing to a bright-eyed soldier about seventeen years of age, who sat looking on with apparent indifference, but who was greatly enjoying the confusion of the ignorant butternut, who had just sense enough to know that something was wrong, but no ingenuity to detect the imposition. I do not justify this money-making trick, but, under the circumstances, its sinfulness is somewhat diminished.

We were then more than a thousand miles from home, surrounded by a bloodthirsty and infuriated mob, robbers of our government, and oppressors of our fellow-men. We were dragged to that prison half-starved and moneyless. Our rations consisted of a bit of spoiled beef not larger than your two fingers, a small slice of coarse corn-bread without salt, and this only twice a day. Whatever more than this we

8

received, we were compelled to buy at fabulous prices. While in Montgomery I became acquainted with a clergyman named Rogers, a member of the Methodist Church South, who had spent many years in the itineracy, and who was a chaplain in the Mexican war. Mr. Rogers was a man of fine talent, vast experience, and apparently of great piety. He had been an intimate friend, in other years, of Parson Brownlow, which circumstance made his acquaintance an interesting one to me. He had been arrested, and, without a trial hurried from his motherless children to this gloomy prison. The old divine gave me an account of some of his sufferings. He had been frequently imprisoned for his loyal sentiments; and in a few instances made hair-breadth escapes from lynching. While he was in prison he preached for us. The gospel sound was glorious to hear, even beneath the cloud that rested upon us. Though in bonds, we could listen to the voice of truth—the truth that makes us free indeed.

I was here again amused and benefited by the ingeniousness of the colored people, of whom so many wiseacres are constantly seeking to prove a natural imbecility. Very often these shrewd observers would anticipate our wants, and bring us such articles as we really most desired. Sometimes an apparently careless lounger would lean himself against our prison-gates, as if to rest himself, and while facing the guards, his skilful fingers would slip a file or a knife through some small aperture to an inside Yankee. These implements were always in demand for the purpose of making rings and trinkets from refuse beef bones. And in case of a contemplated escape from prison, such helps as these are invaluable. It was a constant perplexity to the "Clay-eaters," to see the negroes so well posted on war matters. Though the unhappy race have been down-trodden and abused to an outrageous extent, which nothing short of eternity will adequately punish, yet they are more intellectual and virtuous than the majority of the whites in Secessia. With Anthony Benezett, the philanthrophic Quaker, I sincerely declare that I have found among the negroes as great a variety of talent as among a like number of whites; and I am bold to assert that the notion entertained by some, that they are inferior in their capacities, is a vulgar prejudice, founded on the pride or ignorance of their lordly masters, who have kept their slaves at such a distance as to be unable to form a right judgment of them.

While we lay in this old cotton-shed, thirteen of the prisoners conceived and executed a plan of escape. They succeeded in scaling the walls, and wandered about the country for some time; but being unacquainted with the geographical features of the locality, were all subsequently recaptured, and again brought to the prison. For this attempted escape, several were shot, and others were loaded with huge chains. In the midst of this severe punishment they never once repined, but looked forward with ardent hope to a period when they might again be permitted to defend the ensign of liberty they so dearly cherished. Many who had previously been "conservative" in their views of the peculiar institution, now realized a modification of their sentiments, while the universal conviction seemed to be that this system of human bondage had been the parent source of all our national dissensions.

Captain Troy seemed to derive special delight in practising almost every species of deception upon the defenceless prisoners. He frequently cheered us with assurances that our imprisonment would soon terminate, and that we would be on our way homeward in a short time. All these hopes would as quickly give place to saddening disappointments, for in none of his declarations was there the least shadow of truth! One day he entered and told us that we had been exchanged, and ordered us to immediately prepare for our departure. Then we realized "how deep a gloom one beam of hope enlightens," and in our fancy, already treading the soil of liberty, lost no time in making all necessary preparations to quit the land of chains and cruelty. Nor had we much to prepare—a few moments only, and we stood ready for our exodus. The minutes dragged lazily on that were to introduce us to freedom; but what was our unspeakable vexation and chagrin to learn that we had been the victims of a cruel hoax, perpetrated through sheer diabolism.

One bright and beautiful summer morning, however, legitimate orders came for our instantaneous departure, and, as before, we were soon ready. At eleven o'clock, we stepped aboard the cars, and were soon whirled from this Sodomic city to await the gradual developments of our destiny unknown. Two hundred and fifty miles brought us to the city of Columbus, Georgia, on the Chattahoochee river. The crowd that met us here was composed of remarkably coarse material, and as far as we could perceive, seemed to be an average of the staple human product in that locality. They saluted us with such epithets as "blue-bellied Yankees," "dirty nigger-thieves," &c., exhausting the entire slave-pen vocabulary, the reigning vernacular.

I regret that I am compelled to record the defection of one of our party, whom we had supposed to be in hearty sympathy with us, but, who, as the sequel will show, was co-operating with the enemy. Our first suspicions were aroused by the tender regard shown him by the rebel officials and ladies; but when we came to Columbus, his designs and character became more and more apparent. Of him we shall hereafter speak more at length.

The city in which we had temporarily halted quartered a large force of rebel soldiers, the majority of them better clad than any we had yet met. The place itself, extending one mile and a quarter in the direction of the river, and about half a mile toward the interior, and numbering a population of nearly nine thousand, was a beautiful one. I observed a number of unfinished buildings, erected most probably before the war, but now standing exposed and weather-beaten, with no roofs to protect them from the sun and rain. The people here seemed determined to prolong the war to the last, confident of ultimate success.

CHAPTER VII.

Macon—A Southern Unionist in the Rebel Army—Beneath a Georgia Sun—Secession Speech—Thoughts of Home—Political Prisoners—Horrible Place—Offer of the Gospel—Lieutenant A. P. Collins—Contemplated Escape—Robes of Blood !—Pinning a Federal Soldier to the Ground.

WE were next taken to Macon, Georgia. Traveling by night in box-cars, we had little opportunity to see the country. We were much annoyed on this trip by drunken, profane, and sleepy guards. Their cuffs and curses were almost too intolerable to be borne.

On board the train, however, there was one companionable and intelligent gentleman. I regret that I cannot record his name, for he was a worthy man, and a lover of his country. He related to me many strange inconsistencies of rebeldom. Said he:

"I am here in the army. I was a Douglas Democrat, and opposed this war until my life was threatened. My only alternative was to become a soldier. You may think your case a hard one, sir, but I would readily exchange with you, for then I should not be compelled to fire upon any who rallied beneath the stars and stripes. I was in the Mexican war, and there followed the dear old flag until it floated proudly over the metropolis of the enemy."

He also informed me that he had a family dependent upon him for a livelihood, and complained of a government that paid eleven dollars a month to soldiers, and allowed fifty dollars per barrel to be exacted for flour, and all other necessaries in proportion. Pointing to his coarse shoes, he said:

"These cost me eleven dollars; this flimsy clothing I wear cost ten dollars a yard! Once times were good and we were content and happy; but now my family is suffering, and I know not my own fate. I know not whether you are a Christian or not; but, sir, my hope is in the Lord. He knows my heart; and although I am compelled to do what I believe to be wrong, I feel that God will forgive me for my family's sake."

He was a member of the Methodist Church South, an uneducated man, but honest and humble. He remarked that, if our conversation were overheard, we would both be in danger of immediate death.

The morning light appeared at last, and we

were passing through a level, boggy country, very thinly inhabited.

Soon after dawn, the long, shrill scream of the locomotive announced that we were approaching a place of some note. In a few minutes we were in Macon depot; but of our destiny or doom we knew nothing. At this time there were about six hundred of us. Not until ten o'clock were we permitted to move, hungry and hampered as we were. Then we were taken from the cars, and for the first time set our feet on the traitor-cursed soil of Bibb county, Georgia. In a short time we were driven, like a herd of mules, to the fair-ground, an area of three acres, surrounded by a picket-fence. Within were several large, rough, wooden buildings thrown together for the purpose of holding Yankee prisoners.

It was now the 29th of May, and the noonday heat was intense. They kept us sweltering in the broiling sun for more than two hours, and our sufferings were excessive. Suddenly the attention of the crowd was attracted by a pompous-looking individual, who mounted a stump in the enclosure, and began, with violent gesticulations, to harangue the prisoners.

The substance of this speech is herewith appended, though I confess my inability to transmit it in the *patois* in which it was spoken. It is reported to serve as a specimen of the average of Southern logic and oratory, such as often harried our unwilling ears:

"Prisoners, you have been committed to my charge, and you know that you are invaders of our soil. You have been stealing our property, and running them off to Canada and other places. And when we appealed to you to deliver up our slaves, you passed liberty bills in your States, nullifying a law that had been passed by the legislature, declaring that you would not regard the Fugitive Slave Law. We, in assuming the position we now do, are acting as a safeguard to our slaves, and protecting them as our property—property to which we have the right guaranteed to us by God himself, when he said, 'Servants, be obedient unto your masters.' But you of the North have violated the Word of God, and the Constitution of the once United States. When we asked to secede from you, giving you all your rights, and demanding only our own, your government waged an unholy war against us—have carried it into our country with all its carnage, destruction, and bloodshed. The God of battles is turning all things in our favor, and we are driving your army from our soil—taking your men prisoners, which is your own sad experience. Now, prisoners, you are in my charge, and I am sure you cannot expect me to treat you only as invaders of our soil, and murderers of our countrymen. Notwithstanding all this, I shall try to do the best for you, as poor unfortunate prisoners, that the conscience of a brave and gallant officer would allow him. While you obey my orders strictly, you shall not suffer. But if you disobey them, you must expect to take the consequences."

After this address, embodying so much profundity and wisdom, we were surrounded by a heavy guard, and taken within the guard-lines located on the grounds referred to.

What a dreary spot for our abode, to be endured we knew not how long! A gloomy, dismal pen was to be our habitation. The only shade afforded us was that of a few straggling pine-trees, beneath which we sat at times, brooding over our forlorn and desolate situation. Oh! how wearily passed the days! how sadly the nights! How much did our thoughts revert to the "loved ones at home," and how in imagination did we realize the loneliness of their sorrowing hearts!

Mr. Rogers—before spoken of—came and informed me that a group of men standing at a little distance were from Tennessee and Mississippi, with several of whom he was well acquainted, and asked me to accompany him to where they were. I did so, and learned that there were seven hundred from those States in prison, many of whom had been incarcerated ten or twelve months without any change of clothing, or any comfort to relieve the gloom and monotony of prison life. Among them were lawyers, doctors, and clergymen—persons who had been accustomed to the luxuries of refined society, and the endearments of home. A volume might be written, recording the reflections, sufferings, and experiences of each of these brothers, shut up there in a loathsome prison for faithful adhesion to their loyalty. During that night I slept but little, and said less. My mind was busy in contemplation.

Mr. Rogers conducted me the next night to a long board shanty, which was used as a hospital for the sick and wounded. When I entered, my heart sickened at the awful sight presented. There were confined within that rough wooden enclosure about one hundred sick and dying, with nothing upon which to rest their aching heads. We began the work of contributing as much as possible to their comfort, and of alleviating their sufferings. Most of them were victims of typhoid fever. We had no light to guide us, and the only way we could distinguish the dead from the living was by touch. From time to time was it our painful duty to carry the dead bodies of these, our fellow-prisoners, and lay them upon the grass, where they would often be suffered to remain two or three days, when, being tumbled into rough boxes, they were put upon a dray, and taken we knew not whither. This night was one of gloom, loneliness, and desolation. Our bed was the hard floor, and sleep was too "coy a dame" to be won to conditions so comfortless and lorn. I lay longing for the morning which came at last; and never did I greet the light of day more joyously than the 30th of May, 1862. This was my first night in Macon, Georgia, among the sick, dead, and dying. The place or pen thus used for a hospital, and the ground enclosing it, were of such limited dimensions, that the large number of men found it impossible to be other than exceedingly uncomfortable, and their clothes became infested with bugs and vermin.

The night of the 30th passed wearily away, and ushered in the Sabbath—"soft halcyon on life's turbid waters." The other ministers sought to hold a meeting, and I went to the commandant to obtain his consent, which he granted. With a light heart, I returned to my brother ministers to report my success. A moment after, a note was handed us, stating that no religious services, public or private, would be permitted. After the lapse of a brief period, they concluded to send their own chaplain to preach to us. But we declined to hear him; and I was appointed to give our reasons therefor, which I did as pertinently as possible. They then threatened to force us to become listeners to sentiments which were utterly incompatible with our views of patriotism and Christianity. But they parleyed, and finally desisted from their threats.

It was here that I first became acquainted with Lieutenant A. P. Collins, a gentleman of refinement and culture, and with whom I was destined afterward to share incredible sufferings and perils. He was a religious man, and a graduate of the Ohio Wesleyan University at Delaware, Ohio. He had in his possession a portion of the Old and New Testament, and with this volume it was our wont every day to repair to the shade of the pine-trees for meditation, reading, and prayer. The idea of escaping from our horrible imprisonment, which was every day growing more and more severe, seemed to enter both our minds at about the same time, and we agreed to make it a subject of special prayer. We shrank at the thought of abandoning our comrades in distress; but the hope of life, and the possibility of again striking a blow for justice and right, stimulated us while contemplating such a daring and dangerous project. We looked upon the height of the picket-fence that environed us, the vigilant guard of four hundred men that watched our every movement, and the battery of artillery planted within the enclosure, and our hearts oftentimes sank within us. But our friends were dying around us, and day by day we saw them deposited in rude boxes, hurried for ever from our sight. Once we relinquished our hope of personal deliverance, and determined to remain with our brethren, and, if necessary, die with them. Many who perished there were noble men, though they passed away "unwept, unhonored, and unsung." We now concluded to continue our prayer-meetings in the hospital. In this work we seconded the efforts of the Rev. Mr. Rogers, Dr. Doke, of East Tennessee, and Dr. Fisk, of Illinois. We had not acquainted these gentlemen with our plans. Their names should never die, for

> "Midst fawning priests and courtiers foul,
> The losel swarm of crown and cowl,
> White-robed walked these noble men,
> Stainless as Uriel in the sun."

Their deeds of mercy were too many for record here. No circumstances too repulsive, no night too dark, no duty too onerous, but they were ready for every good word and work. Where suffering and pain were, there were they present to alleviate and sympathize, and many a poor fellow, now gone to his long home, blessed them for prayers and consolations in the night of death.

These noble philanthropists determined to ask for something to mitigate the sufferings of the prisoners, and accordingly made an appeal through a humane surgeon for some bedding on which the dying men might rest. This man carried the message to the commandant, Major Rylander, but that dignitary utterly refused to listen to the appeal. The surgeon then endeavored to awaken his humanity and Christian feeling; but he replied to all this, by saying very emphatically:

"Sir, I have laid off my robe of righteousness, and put on one of blood, and the best way to get rid of these d——d Yankees is to let them lay there and rot."

Such was the conduct of this man Rylander.

We were compelled still to submit to our fate, though we employed every effort in our power to alleviate the sufferings of our dying friends. One case, in particular, attracted my attention. A political prisoner named Foote, who had formerly been a captain of a steamboat plying on the Florida rivers, being suspected as a Union man, was arrested and thrown into prison. He was occasionally visited by his wife, and so careful were the rebels, notwithstanding their boasted superiority, that two guards with loaded guns were invariably detailed to dog the footsteps of this woman. A system of perfect espionage was constantly maintained, and so suspicious were the rebels of each other, that they would not permit a single guard, in any case, to accompany a prisoner. An instance of the most barbarous torture it was ever my lot to behold, I witnessed while here. It was inflicted upon a young man from Illinois, for some offence unknown to me. He was taken and stretched upon the ground, face downward, his legs and arms drawn as far apart as possible, and then pinned to the ground by driving stakes across them; and in this state of terrible torture was he left for twenty-four hours.

Acts like these filled our hearts with the most gloomy forebodings, and we began to seriously deliberate the propriety of consummating our previously contemplated escape. We were about three hundred and fifty miles from the nearest point where the stars and stripes could be reached by water, and two hundred and eighty miles by land. The distance seemed to be insurmountable, to say nothing of the impossibility of surviving the hot weather. But the hope of liberty gave zest to the project, and we determined at once and for ever to abandon the scene of so much horror and misery.

CHAPTER VIII.

Preparing the Way—Dave—Pepper, Matches, and Fish-hooks—Exchange of Clothing—Passing the Guard-lines—Frightened Horse—Halted—Passed—In the Woods—Hidden in the Swamp—Pursued—A Night Journey in the Cane-brake—Manna.

We resolved to select a dark and rainy night to put into execution our long cherished plan, and we waited anxiously for such a night. The morning of the 1st of June, which was the anniversary of my twenty-ninth birth-day, brought with it deep and long forgotten memories of other days.

The next day I was attracted by the movements of the old negro Dave, who was employed in the menial services of the prison. He was evidently well acquainted with our position, and knew all about the state of affairs. As he passed near me, he gave me a significant grin, hung his head in assumed diffidence, and began shoveling among the rubbish with all his might, saying to me as he labored, just loud enough for my ear, but looking all the while at his work:

"You Yankees has jis made about a tousand

of the drefful rebels bite the dust up in Tennessee. I golly, I'se glad!"

"Why, Dave, aren't you a rebel, yourself?"

"No, *sah*, massa, I'se—"

Just here, a straggling rebel official sauntered in sight, and our conversation was interrupted. If any Federal prisoners were discovered holding private consultations with the slaves, there was a death penalty just so adjusted in the martial laws of the Confederacy, as to meet the case. I let the day pass without further effort to see Dave.

The next day, however, finding a favorable opportunity, I asked Dave if he could furnish me three fish-hooks.

"God bless you, massa, yes!"—his eyes snapping fire as he responded.

"Can you get me a tin full of salt, and a paper of pepper?"

"Yes, massa!"

"Can you get me a box of matches?"

"Yes, massa; but how's I gwine to get 'em past the guards?"

"Try, Dave, won't you?"

"Bless your soul, massa, yes!"

I gave him the money, and when his chores were done, he passed out, apparently one of the most stupid darkies I ever saw. Fortunately our conversation was not overheard, and I soon was in possession of the desired articles.

During the day, I visited a Tennesseean—a political prisoner—and proposed to exchange clothes with him, to which he at once assented, suspecting my object. He promised to be true, and reveal nothing. We agreed upon an hour when he should visit my quarters, at which time we were to exchange our clothing. I then informed Collins what I had done, and he made a similar arrangement with another Tennesseean.

Time passed wearily on, and brought the night of the 18th of June,* which was dark and rainy, and promised fairly for our proposed adventure. In due time our United States uniform was exchanged, and we were clad in rebel rags. Our hearts beat high with hope, and we were resolved to escape or perish in the attempt.

About half past eight o'clock, we slowly

* A coincidence here is worthy of notice. On the 18th of June, seven United States soldiers were hung by the rebels at Atlanta, Georgia. They were a part of the celebrated Chattanooga Railroad scouts, sent out on a military excursion by General Mitchell, but who were captured and treated as spies. One of the survivors of the party, Lieut. WM. PITTENGER, gives a full and graphic account of their captivity and imprisonment in a book which every reader of this work should peruse.

crawled out of the prison—Collins a little in the rear.

This, with the exception of crossing the guard-lines, we apprehended would be the most dangerous part of our undertaking, and our movements were consequently slow and cautious. We continued to advance, keeping within whispering distance of each other, until we reached a little clump of pines near the fence, which point we had previously selected as a rendezvous. Here we paused to make further arrangements. We felt certain, now, that if we were discovered, we would be shot. Life for us was only in pressing warily forward. After a minute's consultation, in the lowest whispers, it was agreed that I should take the advance, and that should I be discovered, and shot, he should return to his quarters; but if I succeeded in passing the guard-lines, and reaching our second rendezvous—a thicket of fallen bushes between the guard-lines and picket-fence—I was then to announce my success by a single clap of the hands, which would be a signal for him to follow.

I accordingly lay down on my face, and crept quietly outward through the lines. The intense darkness prevented my seeing a guard, who chanced to be stationed close to my path. I came within six feet of him, and could distinguish that he was reposing carelessly against a tree, playing with the rammer of his gun, the noise of which served to keep me from running against him. It was the most thrilling moment of my life! But I soon got beyond the sound of the clicking ramrod of an enemy whose business it was to shoot just such adventurers as myself, and I began to breathe a little more freely as I neared our second rendezvous. In a few minutes I was safe outside the lines, and snugly hidden beneath the dark foliage of the tangled bushes. Just as I was about giving the signal to Collins, I discovered that I had frightened an artillery horse so much, that he broke loose from his hitching-rack, and in another moment it seemed as if all rebeldom were out in pursuit of him. Now I should be discovered! To run or lie still would be death. An unseen Deliverer gave me presence of mind. I resolved to turn rebel for the time being, and assist in catching the horse. My life depended on the action of that moment. I ordered all the rebels astir, assuming as best I could the arrogant Southern tone of authority, to assist me in securing the animal, and had the gratification of seeing him caught and led away, wondering whether that would be the last of the "catching" to be done that night! Again I started for our place of rendezvous; but being somewhat excited, and the darkness and rain of the night adding to my bewilderment, I ran against an artillery guard, who instantly exclaimed:

"Halt, dar!"

My unseen Protector again aided me, and I once more assumed the rebel tone and manner. I replied, with as much offended dignity as my beating heart would allow:

"Halt, whar?"

"Who are you, sah?"

"Have you been here so long, sir, and don't know me yet? What's this mean, sir? Don't you understand your business, sir?"

"O, yes, sah, I know you, now; you 'long to that thar battallin over thar. Go on, sah!"

Soon after this, I succeeded in reaching our appointed place of meeting, but believing that the confusion of the guards in capturing the frightened horse had prevented Collins from attempting to follow, I went down to the fence alone. Five minutes later, I heard my comrade giving the signal at the outer rendezvous, to which I instantly responded, and in a very few minutes we were both outside the picket-fence, on the dismal banks of the Ocmulgee river.

We traveled fifteen miles before sunrise, and, just at daylight, crossed the river on a railroad bridge, leaving it between us and our enemies. It was a glorious summer morning. The birds, all beautiful and free, were chirping their matin praises. The fields and forests were fragrant with the blessed baptism of dews, and glittered in rare brilliance before the rising sun. All nature was clad in robes of royalty, and voiced to sweet anthems of rejoicing. But we were weary wanderers, homeless and hated, fallen among thieves and robbers in the midst of our native land. As the daylight grew stronger, we resolved to secrete ourselves in the thicket among the croaking frogs, and lie low in the dense undergrowth among the reptiles of the cane-brake. We were destitute of provisions. In our haversacks were the matches, salt, pepper and fish-hooks. We kindled a small fire, and burnt our papers. We did this regretfully, for we had some valuable notes and memoranda among them, but we chose to suffer their positive loss, rather than risk the danger of a recapture with them still in our possession. It was a sad sacrifice, in a solitary sanctuary, on a strange altar. Yet our safety demanded it, and it was done.

Our situation was now both desolate and

dangerous. We were in the midst of a vast cane-brake, the extent and surroundings of which were altogether unknown to us. The tall, straight cane-growths, like steady fingers, pointed upward to a land of liberty on high, and we knew a Present Guide thither, but we were without chart or compass in this lower wilderness.

About three o'clock in the afternoon, we ventured to the road, keeping a vigilant look-out in every direction, dreading the sight of white men, and ardently hoping to see the face of some lowly slave, in order to arrange with our ever-faithful friends and now brothers in common peril and oppression, for something to eat. For a long time we lay silent and watchful beneath the broad leaves of the swamp palm, close by the road-side; but instead of discovering a sympathizing negro to whom we might appeal for food and friendship, what was our bitter disappointment at discovering six armed men on horseback, in pursuit of us! They were making diligent search. We could see them dismount and examine all probable lurking-places to the right and left of the road as they passed along. As they came nearer, we heard their savage curses, and the threatened tortures that awaited us if re-captured. They circled the thicket, and penetrated at every possible angle all about us; but we were so completely concealed that nothing but personal contact would reveal our hiding-place. At one time, our pursuers were within a few feet of us. They must have known we were in that brake, for they lingered within hearing until nightfall. when they abandoned the search. How thankfully beat our hearts as the sound of their horses' hoofs died away in the rearward distance!

There was an advantage to us in what we at first so dreaded—the proximity of these men. We were thereby enabled to overhear their plans of pursuit. They agreed to set watches at certain points on the road, the river, and railroad leading to Darien. We were quite confident we had been betrayed by some cowardly prisoner, and suspected that fellow named Clinton, from Mississippi.

We learned from our pursuers themselves, as they were searching for us, that this traitor of traitors gave the authorities of the prison all the information they desired, for he had played eaves-dropper more than once, rebel and prisoner as he was! He had actually mapped our proposed route, although our scheme was arranged between Collins and myself in whispers.

But we were silently thankful for the information we received, and when we ascertained the plan of pursuit, we fixed our course so as to elude their pickets.

With a thanksgiving and a prayer, we resolved to continue our journey immediately with the beginning of the night. The night was calm and clear. All the sounds that broke the stillness were the hoarse croakings of the frogs, and the distant barking of watch-dogs on the plantations. Looking up to God for guidance, he gave us a glimpse of the North Star, the fugitive's light of hope. We started in a south-east direction, through the cane-brake, traveling part of the time through dirty, stagnant water two feet deep, and sometimes almost to our arms; but it was a venture for life, and we urged our way patiently onward, until we came to water so deep that we were obliged to stop, and wait for the morning. We hailed the day-dawn with delight, hungry and weary as we were, for we had not tasted a mouthful of food since we left the prison. As soon as the grayish light appeared, we discovered that we were on the bank of a swail, beyond which, on a little elevation of land, was one of the richest blackberry fields I ever saw. It was like manna in the wilderness. With these delicious berries we appeased our hunger, and were strengthened for new hardships. The forenoon was one of peculiar beauty to us. We found our Comforting Friend in that sacred retreat, present to cheer our souls and feed our bodies. We rested a few hours, and talked of the goodness of the Lord. Occasionally we would see a strange, unknown reptile glide among the dense ground-foliage, or hear the song of some strange wild-bird. We again started on our way, trying to pass the time pleasantly by remarking the new varieties of vegetation that everywhere met the eye—the wild-flowers, the singular leaves, the swamp-mosses, and the thousand beautiful creations of an Omnipotent Hand, far in the solitudes of Georgia.

CHAPTER IX.

Seeking the Hills—Retreating to the Swamps—Pursued by Bloodhounds—Suffering from Hunger—A Dreary Night—An Answered Prayer—Singular Noise—Lost in the Cane-brake—A Dismal Journey—A Dream—A Surprise—Wanderings and Wearyings in the Wilderness—A Comforter Present—Hope and Cheer—A Cotton-field—A Friend in Need—Negro Music—A Feast in the Night—An Intelligent Slave—Advice to Fugitives.

About two o'clock, we ventured to leave the swamp, and strike out for the low hills, and travel through the pines. It was the 20th of June, and a long day to us. We had scarcely entered the pine forest, when we saw eight men with guns, on the lookout for us, some of whom we had previously seen on the same errand. We instantly retreated to the swamp, yet not before we were discovered. The dogs were instantly put on our track, and in order to break the scent, we again sought the swail, and waded in water to our knees. We passed through the densest portions of the brake, where it stood thick and tall, forming, in places, an almost impenetrable wall of stalks, which we carefully adjusted behind us. After several hours of this cautious traveling and covering our way, we were obliged to lie down among the swamp palm-leaves for rest. We could distinctly hear the baying of the bloodhounds in search of our track, but we felt pretty well assured they would not be able to follow it. The next morning found us wet and weary, and quite chilled by the dampness of our bed. We thought to make our way out to the pine hills, but had hardly concluded to hazard the attempt, when we again heard the hounds nearer than before. We then penetrated yet further into the tangled cane-thicket, for it had become a welcome retreat for us. By patient endurance we again baffled our enemies, only, however, to find ourselves threatened with starvation. We tried to catch fish, but failed. We were even "unlucky" in our attempts to take frogs from the swail with our hooks. Our forlorn situation can better be imagined than described. Cold, wet, hungry, weak from exposure, heart-sick with disappointments, and, worse than all, pursued as criminals by those who should have befriended us, we were almost ready to despair, and lie down to die in the midst of the dismal swamp. I felt that indeed strange changes had occurred in my life; for, only a few months before, I was a free man, surrounded by the kindest of friends, happy in my cottage home, or in my pastoral walks among the people whom I loved. But now I was compelled to flee for life, half clad and half starved, to the heart of a watery wilderness! From our covert of shade we watched the sun go down, and felt the quiet night coming on. Oh! dreary evening! sunless, hopeless, comfortless, and dark! thy memory haunts me still! But we lost not our confidence in God. We knelt in the black water, and prayed. And down through the still night—down through the deep darkness—down through the dense cane-brake—down to our prostrate souls afar in the solitude, came the Blessed Comforter, and we took courage. We thought of the old Jews, compelled to wander about in sheep-skins and goat-skins. We trusted in Elijah's and Elisha's God, and remembered that Daniel had dwelt safely in the den of lions. We were so completely thrown upon God's mercy, that our faith was stronger than ever. We felt that God was nearer in the shadows than in the sunshine—that in bowing in the water of the swamp to pray, we placed our lips nearer to the Infinite Ear than if we worshipped in temples on the mountain.

We spent the entire day, the 21st of June, in this bog. When night came, we tried again to sleep, but were annoyed by a new enemy—a legion strong—the pestiferous musquitoes. During the night, our attention was attracted by a sound like the driving of a stake. We arose and cautiously reconnoitered in the direction from which the noise proceeded. To our surprise, we came upon a small corn-field, containing about two acres, surrounded by a rude fence of pine poles. We trembled at the thought of being so near a human habitation; and after pulling a few stalks of the young corn to eat, we hastened into the thicket, and traveled on. The roots of the corn, cleansed and salted, were eaten with a relish. The sound which had arrested our attention proved to be that produced by an insect of the beetle species, and the painful stillness and solitude of the place, served to make it more impressive than it would otherwise have been. The North Star was our only guide; and shaping our course by its uncertain light, we again resumed our journey. We had not traveled far, however, until we became completely bewildered in the cane-brake. The sluggish water spread on every side, the thick cane and underbush so mingled and commingled, that it was impossible to move in any direction. Again we concluded to tarry for the daylight; and breaking a few cane-stalks, and laying them on the ground near a mossy log, for a bed, we tried to sleep. We were frequently disturbed in the night by prowling animals, but none of them was so terrible to think of as our human pursuers. Judging it best to guard against all surprises from man or beast, we agreed to sleep and stand sentinel alternately until morning. Thus we relieved and rested each other that memorable night.

It was a welcome day-dawn to us. For two hours I had stood guard over Collins, watching the stars mirrored on the smooth waters about our feet, and it was a glorious sunrise to us that chased the shadows and images away, and flooded our gloomy retreat with the light of morning. Again we started onward, taking the sun for our guide. The water grew gradually more and more shallow, and the brushwood thicker. Berries became scarcer, and our sufferings from hunger increased with every step. We were that day wandering weary, footsore, and heart-heavy, where in all probability, human foot had never trod before:

"In the dark fens of the dismal swamp,
The hunted Yankees lay;
We saw the fire of the midnight camp,
And heard at times the horses' tramp
And the bloodhounds' distant bay.

"Where hardly a human foot would pass,
Or a human heart would dare,
On the quickening turf of the green morass,
We crouched in the thick and tangled grass,
Like wild beasts in their lair."

On we pressed, amid the wild voices of the dark cane forest. Our progress was slow. By-and-by, as we came upon a mossy log, we tarried and tried to rest our aching heads. We soon fell asleep, being overcome by fatigue. I dreamed of my loved ones at home—of watchful eyes and praying voices in our behalf. I saw the old familiar hill-slope before my cottage door, the orchard, the fields, and, better than all, the friends of other days, and myself among them—all happy at the old homestead in free Ohio. Some hovering angel must have come and held the picture before my eyes, for I was in raptures of delight! Suddenly I was aroused from my slumbers by the tread of some animal, I knew not what. As I stirred, it hastened into the dark foliage and was gone. I awakened my comrade and told him it was morning. He was surprised to think he had slept so long, and both of us were greatly refreshed. Again we prayed and pressed onward for home and friends, and for a sight of the Stars and Stripes. We had decided on keeping steadily on in a south-easterly course until we reached some point on the sea-coast then in our possession. The sun beamed hotly over our heads. We traveled as fast as possible all day, hoping that we might find some negro—none else in that region were human beings—and through the aid of slaves get something to eat, for we were actually starving. We captured a frog that day, and divided the precious morsel between us, with thanksgiving. At night we lay down, but hunger and faintness prohibited repose. We longed for morning. We gazed upward to the twinkling stars, praying them to speed faster through the firmament, and let the sun arise. At length the blushing morn appeared. I hailed it as the dawn of an eventful day, for now we must seek and obtain food, or perish in the swamp. The idea of falling into the hands of our enemies chilled our very souls. We thought to die alone, and "let the dead bury the dead" in the wilderness, rather than suffer ourselves to be recaptured and tortured to death by inches, to gratify the jeering, jabbering multitudes. But the day was come when something more must be ventured for life's sake. At last dawn came, and again we fell upon our knees and asked for wisdom and direction in the hour of need.

Rising comforted and strengthened, we changed our course, and pressed forward, expecting to emerge from the cane-brake and find a plantation where there were slaves. The undergrowth was so dense that we could with difficulty make about one mile per hour. The day was fast passing away, and so was our strength. At about three o'clock in the afternoon, we sat down, almost in despair, and held a council, when we decided that nothing but the hand of the Lord could deliver us. Again we bowed ourselves before Him, and rose refreshed both in mind and body. Our steps were elastic—our hearts gladdened, and we hurried onward, under the conscious protection of God.

Suddenly, I heard the barking of a dog not far distant. We paused and listened. It was not a bloodhound. Collins, being a little deaf from the effects of terrific artillery-firing at Shiloh, did not, at first, catch the sound. Now we knew that help was near. We quickened our pace, and in a few minutes heard the voices of some negro men. A few steps further, and we came in sight of a cotton-field, which we approached by walking in the water of a small brook that flowed in that direction. With great caution, we neared the field, in which there were twenty-five negroes at work ploughing cotton. Most of the men looked old and toil-worn. While we were reconnoitering our ground, I observed an old, gray-haired man nearing the fence with his furrow, and when he paused a moment to scrape his plough, before returning across the field, I rapped on a rail, which instantly drew his attention. When I caught his eye, I beheld an intellect and a sympathy languaged there which gave me hope. I approached the old man with trembling step and faltering voice, I know, for there was danger of communicating with some excitable and treacherous slave—although such are rare cases—yet I ventured to speak to my wondering auditor. I approached that cotton-field, half famished as I was, with many of my Virginia prejudices against the negroes, for I had been taught to regard them as unreliable and stupid. But I felt that death was in the swamp, and life *might* be in the cotton-field.

"Well, uncle," said I, "I am traveling through your country, and I am very ragged, as you see. I don't wish to call on white folks in this condition, and I am very hungry. Could you get me something to eat?"

"Oh, yes, massa! God bless you! all you

want; but go back! go back!" he continued, waving his hand, as if to hurry me back to our hiding-place; "go back, massa! they's after you wid de houns and de horses! Do you see dat ole cabin up dar, in dat field? To-night, just at 'leven o'clock, come to dat cabin, massa, and I'll gin you all de supper you want. Now, go back! go back, massa!"

"Uncle, you won't bring anybody with you, will you?"

"Why, God bless you, massa; *I knows you! I knows you!*"

"Now, uncle, what do you know about me?"

"Why, you's one of dem Yankees dat broke away from Macon prison, massa. *I knows you!* God bless you!"

"Well, uncle, don't tell that to anybody, will you?"

"Tinks *I* tell anybody, massa, when all I's got in dis worl' depends on ye? No, no, massa! But go back! go back, till 'leven o'clock! mine, now, massa!" and he started after his plough, for by this time the other hands were approaching. I went back, and reported the prospects to my comrade. We concealed ourselves in the thick brush to await the appointed hour. Just at dusk, the slaves unhitched their mules, finished up their rows, and started for their cabins, singing:

"We'll soon be done wagging with the crosses,
We'll soon be done wagging with the crosses,
We'll soon be done wagging with the crosses,
And wing, and wing, and wing with the angels,
And den wing with the angels,
In the New Jerusalem!"

It was weird, eccentric music, but really the most thrilling I had ever heard, as it rose through the still evening air in rich, mellow accord from the voices of the whole company of slaves returning to their humble homes for supper and rest. I thought, how little the people in the North knew about these *crosses!* and I silently but fervently prayed for the day to hasten when all these weary ones might find the liberty for which they sang and suffered.

The hours passed slowly away, but at length the appointed hour of eleven o'clock drew nigh. We left our retreat, and advanced with the utmost caution, until we came within thirty yards of the cabin, when we lay down in a brier-path to watch for whatever movements might occur. For a few minutes we were kept in suspense, not feeling fully satisfied whether friend or foe might advance to meet us. Soon, however, the faithful old negro came to the designated trysting-place. He was evidently alone. He walked round and round the cabin, looking and waiting for us, and on seeing us not, seemed greatly disappointed. When we had assured ourselves that no one was with him, and that he was true, we arose from our concealment, and walked to the cabin. He was rejoiced to see our confidence in him, and was as thankful to give, as we were to receive, the rich repast he had prepared for us. Our supper consisted of corn-bread, smoked bacon, and boiled cauliflowers. He also brought us a bottle of sweetened water. What a feast! Never did I partake of food with such a relish. We received it as directly from the hand of Him who "heareth the young ravens when they cry." Being assured by our old friend that we were perfectly safe, we tarried after supper several hours, conversing on the state of our country, and receiving advice as to the manner of proceeding on our journey. As the venerable man talked to us, telling us how to escape to our homes and friends, sharing his sympathies and his means with us poor destitute wanderers, my old prejudices of caste were entirely obliterated. Beneath that dark brow was the mind of a man, and within that slave's bosom beat a brother's heart. I could have embraced him as my father.

"Now, massa," said he, as we were about to separate until all true friends shall meet in heaven, "now do jis as I tells you, and you'll git away. You keep dis pine-ridge straight on through massa's plantation for five mile. Dis ridge goes clean to de coast. It's 'bout three hundred mile to de coast by de Ocmulgee riber. The Ocmulgee flows into de Altamaha, and Darien is at de mouth of de Altamaha, and you'll find lots of de Yankees dar."

The old man understood the times. His knowledge of the war, with all its recent and important movements, was thorough and accurate, although he was careful and somewhat reticent, even in his communications to us. In order to test his professed knowledge of us, and to ascertain all we could relative to our pursuers, we plied him with various questions.

"Well, uncle," said we, "I suppose you know we are running from the conscript?"

"No, sah, I knows you is the Yankees what broke out o' jail at Macon, dat's what I knows."

"You're right, uncle. Now what do you know about this war?"

"I doesn't know much about it, sah; only I knows dat dey say, if de Yankees whips, de darkies all be free, but if dese har rebels whips, den we be slaves."

"Which do you prefer should gain the day?"

"Why, God bless you, massa! does you tink I's a fool? Course, I wants you to whip."

"You say they are hunting us; how many have they after us?"

"I doesn't know jis zacly; but I knows dat tree men come to massa day 'fore yesterday for to git a bloodhound to hunt Yankees with what runned away from Macon prison."

I confess that the thought of being pursued by bloodhounds was horrifying in the extreme; and notwithstanding we had already seen two large packs at different times upon our track, the possible death by these fierce monsters in this wilderness made my blood run cold.

Our further conversation gave us a full and satisfactory knowledge of our route, and was delineated by our sable friend, as we had afterward reason to know, with perfect geographical accuracy. We asked him that in case we should be pursued by the bloodhounds, what means we should employ to bewilder them. This was no new subject to him. He, in common with his fellow-bondmen, had seen too many instances in which these brutes had been employed in capturing fugitives, not to know their nature, as well as the plans adopted to elude them. He told us when the dogs followed us in the cane-brake, in order to prevent them from keeping the trail, we should travel as much as possible in the water; but if we should be closely pursued, to leave the cane-brake, and take to the Ocmulgee river. He assured us that the dogs were fearful of the alligators with which that river abounded, and that the slaves were taught that alligators would destroy only negroes and dogs. He didn't believe it himself, although his master thought he did. He added:

"If dem houns gits close on to you, why you jis git a long pole, and hop about twenty feet, if you kin. You do dis four or five times, and whenever you light, why jis put some pepper in de holes what your heels make, and when de houns come, dey lose dar scent, and den dey goes a snufflin and a snufflin roun', and bymeby dey snuffles up dat 'ar pepper into dar nostrils, and den dey'll go chee! chee! chee! and dat'll be de last dem dogs can do dat day."

This piece of information, and the manner in which it was conveyed, accompanied as it was by violent gyrations of the body, and an exact imitation of dog-sneezing, was very amusing;

and though surrounded by forbidding circumstances, we indulged in an audible smile.

From this man we first learned of a complete organization among the negroes, for the purpose of aiding fugitives in making their escape. It was similar to an institution which I had often heard of as existing in the Northern States, under the name of "Underground Railroad." The officers of this Southern Underground Railroad, on which we were glad to take passage, were the slaves of the different plantations, who were thoroughly acquainted with their duties, and were very suspicious lest they should be imposed upon. When we inquired how these men should know us, he told us that he would arrange that matter, so that we need have no fears, but to submit ourselves to their guidance, and all would be well.

We traveled that night through the plantation belonging to the master of this black man. We reached the woods just a little before the dawn of day, and here we lay down until a faint light streamed in from "the windows of morning," when we resumed our journey. All was lone and silent. The wood through which we went, with its alluring depths—the verdant moss beneath our eager feet—each blossom-laden, fragrant bough—and the bearded grasses that shook in the wind,—all gave me their secret sigh. All the sweet land around—the distant hill—the distant shore, said, "Redeem me from my chains!"

CHAPTER X.

Pursued by Horses, Hounds, and Men—Another Night in the Cane-brake—An Alligator—A Pleasant Disovery—The Pass-word—Slaves at Work—A Negro Supper—Important Information—A Panther—A Chase to avoid a a Chase—Bloodhounds Again—Fourth-of-July Dinner—Dismal Night in the Ruins of a Meeting-house.

WHILE thus making our way through the forest, we fancied we heard the sound of pursuers, and were once more obliged to take refuge in the dismal, but now welcome cane-brake. Just where we entered the swamp, the water was very shallow, and, consequently, afforded us but poor protection from the bloodhounds, whose peculiar cries we expected to hear every moment. We therefore made our way with as much haste as possible far into our miry retreat, where the depth of mud and water secured us from the scenting of the fearful animals and their bloodthirsty masters.

Presently we came upon a stream of water, which, diverging from the river at a point above, made a circuit, and fell into the river again at a point below us, thus converting the area it embraced into an island. The water looked deep, and we did not relish a soaking, after having our clothes dried during our stay in the woods. But once on the island, our safety was insured for there was no ferry-boat, nor even a skiff, in that silent, murky swamp, by which our would-be captors might cross over. Besides, we had seen too many hardships to be frightened by trifles, and we therefore plunged boldly in, my brave comrade taking the advance, and soon reached the island.

That night, June 24th, we made ourselves a bed on the banks of the Ocmulgee, by cutting down the canes which grew around us in luxuriance. We also kindled a fire, after screening the spot so effectually as to prevent its light reaching the eyes of any foe; and by its cheering flames we partially dried our wet and ragged clothing. Casting ourselves upon our rude couch, we watched the beautiful stars in the distant realm on high, and listened to the murmurs of the crystal stream that was protecting us from pursuit, until at last we fell into a deep slumber. Just before closing our eyes, we heard, at some little distance below us, a noise resembling that which might be made by a huge log, one end of which was caught upon a sand-bank, and the other playing loosely in the stream. But we were too sleepy to suppose that there was any danger indicated by the odd sound, and we paid no attention to it.

Protected by that God who watched Hagar in the wilderness, we slept peacefully until day-dawn, when we were suddenly aroused by the most terrific noise I had ever heard. It resembled the sound of a heavy steam-whistle, though not quite so loud nor shrill. Remembering at the moment a description by the Rev. Joshua Boucher, who had traveled in Georgia, of the bellowing of an alligator, I at once concluded that this must be one. Stepping from my tent, or rather cane-hut, I had ocular demonstration of the fact, for there, only a short distance from me, lay the hideous reptile in all his ugliness. Thinking it about time that one or the other of us should change quarters, I threw a chunk at him. He took the hint, and crawled away into the water, only, however, to return in about ten minutes to his old post, where, opening his fearful jaws, and keeping them so until they were covered with flies, he snapped them together with a report that chilled our blood. This was Wednesday morning, June 25, and we intended to remain all day in the swamp, for the river was lined with boys and negroes. During the afternoon, we espied a skiff on the opposite side, and laid several plans to obtain possession of it, but they were all frustrated. This proved to be a blessing, however, for, while making our last attempt, we were seen by an old negro, who seemed to recognize us immediately. From this lowly slave we learned that the river was guarded for miles, to prevent our escape. Our pursuers were on the watch for us all the way to Hockinsville. This newly-found friend pointed out to us our only path of escape, and appointed a spot where he would meet us at midnight, and bring us some food. We blessed the negro, and, following his directions, reached the place of refuge, where we anxiously awaited his second appearance. But the hour passed on, and so did several more, but he came not. He had, doubtless, been seized by the patrollers.

The sun of the 26th found us still pressing forward. We had gotten thus far, like the old apostles, with "neither scrip nor staves," but we felt that God was with us, and his servants, the poor, downtrodden slaves, helped us on. Whenever we met one of the latter, who replied to our question, "Can't dis yer day," he was a friend, but unable to assist us on account of the patrollers. If one answered, "I know you," he was posted, and all was well.

We passed the night in the pine woods, I remaining awake, and guarding my friend, Collins, who was completely worn out. During the next day, we made a good distance, in spite of numerous difficulties. By the 28th, our rebel clothing was well nigh worn off us, and our hunger began to increase terribly. In the evening, we came upon some slaves in a field, among whom were several females, about eighteen or twenty years of age. The latter were almost naked, having nothing on them save a very short skirt, fastened round the waist, and held in its place by straps, which passed over the shoulders. All the upper portion of the body, and about three-fourths of the nether limbs, were thereby exposed. None of their complexions were black, while one or two of them were nearly white. We agreed with these slaves to hide ourselves in a neighboring lane until night, when they promised to bring us food. Shortly after, one of them brought us the unwelcome intelligence that we were in danger, and warned us to again take to the swamp, which was some half a mile away. This we did, and after wandering some time along the edge thereof, sat down at last beside a clear crystal spring, in which were sporting numbers of beautiful fish. We could hear the negroes singing in the field—which exercise was a signal we understood to mean that we should lie still until it ceased, when we might safely venture out to the lane—until about nine o'clock, when all became quiet. By midnight we returned to our designated hiding-place, where we were soon joined by a black man and one of the girls, a beautiful, modest creature we had seen in the corn-field. They brought us fat meat, corn-bread, greens, and "bonny-clabber," which was a welcome sight to us. During the conversation we held with these negroes, we learned that their master had gone to the war, leaving them in the charge of an overseer. We ascertained, also, that "the Yankees" had possession of Darien, on the coast, and that, in consequence, the slaves had been removed into the interior of Georgia. Close by there were three hundred rice-farm hands encamped, who were in a starving condition, having been driven to the interior of the State by their masters, in order to prevent confiscation, and being unable to make a living for themselves. Our humble friends informed us that if we continued straight on we would reach Darien in two days, provided we exercised due caution to avoid the patrollers, who, since our escape from Macon, had been searching for us vigilantly. The night was well nigh all spent in conversation with these slaves, and we had not got much further on our way, when the dawn broke upon us, compelling us to leave the road and take to the pines. We were subsequently obliged to leave even these, and plunge once more into the more friendly swamps.

After our slender stock of provisions was exhausted, we became exceedingly hungry, and the day passed away without our obtaining even so much as a frog or fish. We slumbered all the night, which was chilly and damp, in the cane-brake. A fire which we had kindled, we were obliged to extinguish, for fear that its light might point out our refuge to some enemy. During the stilly hours that followed, we were once disturbed by a strange noise, which, I subsequently ascertained, in a conversation with Rev. Dr. Kost, must have been made by a panther.

The next day, being terribly fatigued and hungry, we resolved to make an attempt at replenishing our commissary department. The sun came up bright and very hot, and our journey through the swamp-palms was indeed a toilsome one; but these self-same palms secured us against our pursuers, and we therefore did not complain.

An effort that we made shortly after to leave

the marsh, discovered to us our pursuers, and we were once more forced back to our muddy asylum, where we concealed ourselves beneath a muscadine vine until twelve o'clock. While so concealed, a strange noise fell upon our ears, and presently we saw a black man coming directly toward us, blowing a horn to call swine. When he was about thirty feet from us, we called to him, with the expectation of learning from him at what points on the river the guards were stationed, and also of obtaining from him something to eat.

Upon being first hailed, he exclaimed, "Don't know you, sah!" and when, stepping from my concealment, I called to him a second time, he seemed terrified. The next instant he fled madly away from us, we pursuing him desperately, in order to secure him, and thus save ourselves from new pursuers. But, notwithstanding the fact that he carried a bushel basket half filled with corn upon his back, he distanced us. Once he stumbled in a swail, and sent the corn and mud all over himself, but he quickly regained his feet, and was soon after lost to our view.

We were now indeed in peril; and very shortly afterward, the wild bay of the blood-sounds rang upon our ears through the murky

"We beheld the glistening eyes of the hounds, saw their long tongues lolling from between their powerful jaws, and saw their large, terrible teeth shining like pearls."—Page 139.

air of the morass. Nearer, clearer, deadlier came the dreadful sounds, and we crouched in our retreat, expecting every moment to see the ferocious animals bounding upon us. But, thank God for his watchful mercy, the brutes, misguided by a stratagem which the negroes had taught us how to execute, were deceived, and we had the infinite delight of seeing them dash into the stream, swim to the other side, and then, renewing their fierce cries, bound away, closely followed by fifteen human blood-hounds mounted on fleet horses. The peril was not past yet, however, for, finding themselves thrown from the scent, the well-trained brutes soon came back to the stream, recrossed to the side we were on, and coming to our old track, lay down, snuffing and panting, not a hundred yards from us. Think of that, reader! Peeping through the canes we beheld the glistening eyes of the hounds, saw their long tongues lolling from between their powerful jaws, and saw their large, terrible teeth shining like pearls.

Their savage masters stood on the bank of the swail cursing us, and threatening what they would do if they retook us. Once more the God of our fathers stretched forth His arm and delivered us, for, hearing them post their men, we struck away from them in a northern direction, and shortly had the satisfaction of leaving them some fifteen miles in the rear.

Onward, onward we pushed, until so overcome with fatigue that we were fain to stretch ourselves upon the sand and sleep. This was July 3d. The succeeding day—the Fourth—broke upon us bright and beautifully, and we sped forward with all the power of our limbs. We came at last to a very scanty corn-field, which, as we learned from the slaves who attended to it, yielded only about two and a half bushels to the acre. Cotton was the staple in that region, and with it were bought all the necessaries of life. Poor as was the corn, however, we carefully confiscated some roasting-ears, on which, with half of a frog, we made our Fourth-of-July dinner, thanking our Divine Preserver for the gift. The remaining half of the frog was carefully reserved, with some corn, for a future meal.

The morrow was cloudy and cool. We were now drawing near to the coast, for, as we went along, we espied a turtle belonging to a species that lived only in salt water. His shell was extremely beautiful, and would, doubtless, have been very valuable had we thought about dollars and cents; but some berries, which we found, were of far greater worth to us at that time.

Night found us still wandering in the land of rattlesnakes, scorpions, and traitors. Next day, while hunting a sweet-potato patch for a stray root or two, we saw a negro man, to whom we did not, however, get a chance to speak. Fearing that he might not, perhaps, be friendly, we once more betook ourselves to the pines, where, although we did not know it at the time, we were hotly pursued. Soon afterwards, the rain fell in torrents, while the thunder rolled in heavy peals, and the lightning played sharply about us. When evening came, we were soaking wet, and chilled through; and coming to an old dilapidated building, that was overgrown with Spanish moss, and seemed as though it had been uninhabited for many a year, we hurried into it. By the aid of the lightning, we found that it was nearly filled with half-wild goats, which, on our arrival, hastily evacuated the premises, leaving us in free and undisputed possession. The structure was nothing more than an old church, with some rude benches in one end, and a ruined chancel at the other. I here found some leaves of a Bible, upon which I pillowed my head for the night, and slept the more sweetly that I did so. Adjoining this church was a graveyard, containing some rough tombstones, beneath which slept the dead ones of many years, all unconscious of the events passing above their heads.

The following day we left our retreat, and continued our flight in the midst of a terrible storm. About three o'clock, we discovered a sweet-potato patch, but it had been completely stripped of every root. That night, unable, on account of having got our matches wet, to kindle a fire, we slept in a corn-field, pulling the dried stalks over us to partially shelter us from the descending rain. The next day, we resumed our flight, or rather our wading, for every rivulet was swollen to a good-sized creek. In endeavoring to cross a turbid stream upon the "giddy footing" of a loose log, we were precipitated into twelve feet of water, and were obliged to swim to the other shore, grateful that we escaped with nothing worse than a ducking.

CHAPTER XI.

Nearing the Coast—Dangerous Predicament—Suspicious Company—A Fugitive Conscript—Clay-eating Officials—The Squire—Arrested—Mess No. 44, *alias* Mr. Meeser—Acquitted—Placed under Guard—In Chains Again—A Forced March—Before the Court—A Union Speech in Dixie—Better Fare—Southern Superstition—A Slave at Prayer.

WE were now within thirty-five miles of the coast, and here the river took a direct turn eastward, by which we knew that we were on the direct road to Darien. Two miles further on, we suddenly came upon some houses. Men and women were passing almost within hailing distance; but caution forbade us revealing ourselves, and so we attempted to regain the swampy thicket. On our way thither, we passed a field in which were a number of geese; and so strong was the temptation to ascertain whether goose was as palatable as frog, that we halted, and concealing ourselves, wearily awaited the fall of night, intending to make a foray by starlight. But by four o'clock a heavy thunder-storm came up; and dreading to be again wet, we made our way to an old waste-house near by where, shortly, much to our surprise, in came two men, one rather old, and the other young. They inquired where we were from. Collins, whose fictitious name was Compton, told them that we lived in Pulaski county, Georgia; that we had been driven by the Yankees from Darien, and were now on our way home. We were in a hurry to get there before the conscripts left for the seat of war, in order that we might go with our own boys.

This they thought was all true; and when the rain ceased, we kept up the deception by walking along the road with them. They soon after struck off into a by-road, and when we had gone a little further on, and thought ourselves safe, we turned our footsteps back towards Darien. Just as we turned, we were hailed by a man all clothed in rags, whose appearance indicated that he might have been hiding in the swamp for months. He quickly joined us, and entered into conversation. He opposed the war violently; and judging from this that he was merely acting a part, I determined to be "secesh."

"I don't understand," said he, "this tarnal war!"

"Why! you're not a Yankee, are you?" I asked.

"Oh, no!" he replied; "but I don't understand it."

"Why," resumed I, "don't you know that the Yankees are coming down here to free our negroes?"

"Darn the tarnal niggers!" was the rejoinder; "I ain't got any."

"But they will confiscate our land."

"Well, I haven't got no land, so they can't hurt me. Another thing, they say they're fighting for the old flag we all loved."

Rallying myself, I answered:

"They're all abolitionists; and if you and I don't fight, these negroes will be freed among us."

"Well, now, gentlemen," said our new companion, "if you'll hear me a minute, without getting mad, I'll tell you all about my case. I'm a conscript, and I've got to go soldiering for eleven dollars a month. If I'd get a jean like that of yours"—pointing to an old cotton coat that I wore—"I'd have to pay eleven dollars a yard for it. These shoes I've got on cost ten dollars; corn-meal is two dollars and fifty cents per bushel, and salt one dollar per pound. Now, how in the d——l can a man soldier under them circumstances?"

I felt myself completely beaten; but still fearing a catch somewhere, I resolved to try the fellow again.

"Why, you're a regular-built Yankee!" I exclaimed, "and ought to be taken up, and if I had my way, you would be."

At this he changed the subject, and we told him the Pulaski county story. He then invited us to his house to get something to eat, to which, of course, we had to consent. While there enjoying our meal, which consisted of corn-bread and sour milk, and watching him closely all the time, in marched fifteen conscripts. They immediately seized the master of the house, and put him under a heavy guard. Here was a new dilemma, and I winked at my comrade to answer all questions, as I was fearful that if both of us undertook the task, some fatal mistake might occur. He did so, and succeeded remarkably well, for he was shrewd and quick at perception. I stood carelessly by the fire, drying the only stocking I had, and playing the idiot to what I thought perfection. The intruders were dressed savagely, their heads being covered with rudely-made caps of coon-skin, the tail of the animal hanging down their backs. Several of them were eating the clay which has so often been noticed by travellers in the South.

These miserable creatures despatched one of their number on a jenny, who shortly after returned, bringing with him the "squire," a long, lanky, knock-kneed man, with hollow eyes and lantern jaws. He had a law-book tucked under his arm, to give weight, I suppose, to his appearance. This dignitary (?) stepped to me, and began questioning me with much official haughtiness, in fact so offensively, that I became enraged at last, and throwing off my assumed character of an idiot, exclaimed:

"Who *are you?*"

"I'm the *squiah,* sir, the *squiah!*" he replied, in his half negro dialect, and in exceedingly pompous tones.

"Well," said I, "the people who made a squire of you must have been very short of material. But, sir squire, what is your business here?"

"To hold a trial over *you;* that thar's my bis'nis here."

I looked the ignoramus sternly in the face, as I rejoined:

"Well, sir, if you undertake to '*hold a trial*' over Pulaski county citizens, we'll make you smoke for it."

My determined manner nonplussed him considerably, and turning to a companion, who seemed to be a conscripting officer, he said:

"I don't want nuthin' to do with these yer tarnal fellers, fur they know 'emselves, I golly!"

The conscripting officer, however, was not so easily turned aside, for failing to induce the "*squire* to hold a trial on us," he sent a message to the deputy sheriff, and that high functionary came promptly to the rescue of the "Confederacy," and arrested us. The squire having thus shifted this responsibility, regained his courage, and said to us, fiercely:

"Now, then, you're arrested, and you've got ter tell us who you are, and whar from."

"Ah! we're prisoners now, and you may find out all you want to know if you can," was our reply.

We were forthwith searched, the result of which was the finding of a slip of paper in one of my pockets with "*Mess No.* 44" written on it. Not one of our captors could read; and when I asked for a written copy of the charges against us, they were completely dumbfounded. The "squire," with a kind of glorification in his tones, said:

"A bill, you tarnal fool! I can't write, I golly!"

My comrade was asked if he could read and write, and on his saying yes, the card was handed to him to decipher. The crowd clustered around, and when he assisted them in spelling out the word upon it, one cute fellow exclaimed:

"Meeser! Meeser! that's it!"

"Yes, that's it," bawled another, who had thrown himself on a bed; "Mr. Meeser, I golly! John Meeser, what lives up in Pulaski county, and keeps a grocery, and sells good whiskey, I golly."

Here was our salvation; and starting forward, I harangued my wondering auditors with all the eloquence at my command, appealing, and threatening, and reasoning by turns. The result was that we were acquitted, the "squire" himself announcing it in the following laconic style:

"You're clar, I golly!"

The night setting in with a heavy storm of rain, again we were all compelled to remain in the house together. We, ourselves, pretended to sleep, and heard the rebels several times remark:

"How sound these men sleep! None but innocent men could sleep that way."

"Shortly after midnight, we made an attempt to escape, but, opening the wrong door, we found ourselves in another room, which was tenanted by some of the conscripts. In an instant all were awake, and we were once more seized. Several of them accused us of being devilish Yankees, and urged hanging as the best course to pursue. Others of them still believed us to be what we had represented ourselves. This division of opinion resulted in the deputy sheriff ordering us to be taken from the house under a guard of six men with loaded muskets. He followed us out, telling us as we walked along, that we must go into close confinement. We could not realize what he meant, but we soon learned, for within ten minutes we were chained together with a huge chain. One end was twined round my neck, and secured with a large padlock, while the other end was placed in like manner about Collins' neck.

There, in the midst of ruthless foes, a thousand miles away from home and its endearments, we stood wet, ragged, and forlorn; chained, yes, chained together, like felons, like oxen, like wild beasts. Had it not been for the comforting spirit of God, I am certain that I should have sunk at this juncture with despair; for in fancy I could see my wife and my little ones in their peaceful cottage, fondly asking when the absent loved one would return. "Ah!" thought I, "when, indeed, shall I be joined to you once more, darlings? Shall it be on this earth, or

"One end of the chain was twined round my neck, and secured with a large padlock, while the other end was placed in like manner about Collins's neck."—Page 150.

shall it be in that better land where man's inhumanity to man makes no one mourn?"

In the morning, our merciless captors, forming on either side of us, and also in our rear, forced us to march forward. My wounded foot and hand pained me very much, and it was with the utmost difficulty that I could walk. The disparity, also, in the height of my comrade and myself—I being much taller than he—caused me to give him a severe jerk at every step. So fatigued and dispirited did we at last become, that we threw ourselves down, and refused to go any further. At this our captors threatened to shoot us. We were not to be intimidated thus, however, and the ruffians were at last obliged to obtain a rickety old wagon, in which we were carried some distance. After traveling forty-five or fifty miles, we arrived at the town of Jackson, Georgia, where the people had already heard of our approach. On reaching the place, we were allowed to seat ourselves on a Captain Smith's porch, until a court could be convened for our trial. The jury was composed almost entirely of old men, and while they were preparing for their assumed duties, our guards were off trying to hunt up some whiskey. But as the latter article was worth eight dollars a pint, their efforts were not likely to meet with much success. This was fortunate for us, as, if they should obtain enough of the vile compound to intoxicate themselves, they would most likely kill us on their return.

The court soon being prepared to proceed, I was the first arraigned. We had resolved to tell the truth concerning ourselves, no matter whether we should die for it or not, and so I addressed the court as follows:

"May it please the court, I was born in Rockbridge county, Virginia, but early in life removed with my father to Ohio, and settled in Shelby county, where he raised his family of six sons and three daughters. Of this family, I am the youngest member, except one. Early in life I commenced a public career, which I followed until I heard of the bombardment of Fort Sumpter—until I heard that a league of men, banded together for the express purpose of destroying the best government on God's earth,—had dragged our glorious old banner down into the dust, and trampled it beneath their feet, and finally fired it from a cannon's mouth, in order that no vestige of it might remain. Then I remembered that my grandsire had fought under that holy banner at Bunker Hill; that he was present on the field, when Molly Pitcher, stripping the uniform from the stiffening limbs of her dying husband, assumed his command, and drove the enemy back. I also remembered that, in 1812, my father, leaving at home all his loved ones, took the field in defence of the Stars and Stripes. I have heard my mother say—God bless her! she is now in heaven—that her husband and six brothers were in the army at the same time. Now, gentlemen, do not think I will waive any part of the facts in the case. The son of pious parents, I was always taught to speak nothing save the truth; but, on the day we were arrested by these gentlemen, if I dare call them such, I gave my first denial of the positive truth. We both endeavored to deceive you. And why? Because we knew that our lives were not safe, if you should learn who we really were."

(Here a voice said, "No, by golly, they're not safe, *now!*")

"Gentlemen, be that as it may," continued I, "I will speak my last words with courage, and they shall be truthful words. When this war broke out, I was engaged at my profession in Cincinnati, Ohio; but I felt, and I avowed it at Heaven's altar, that I could be nothing else than a United States soldier. I accordingly volunteered to join my loyal countrymen already in the field.

"On March 4th, we left Paducah, Kentucky, and on the 13th, we landed on Pittsburg Hill. I contended with all my heart and might against Beauregard's skirmishers for several days; but I was finally overpowered by numbers, captured, and taken to Corinth. From there I was taken to Columbus, Mississippi, from there to Montgomery, Alabama, and from thence to Macon, Georgia. On the night of June 18th, in company with my comrade, I broke from the guard-house at the latter place, ran your guard-lines, and escaped. Since then we have been fed and assisted by your negroes, until now we are in your power.

"In conclusion, gentlemen, I would say, shoot me, hang me, cut my throat, kill me in any way you please. But, know you, that in so doing, you kill a United States soldier, who glories in these chains!" I shook my chains as I finished.

In an instant there was an uproar, some demanding that our chains should be removed, and others swearing that they should not. The matter was settled by the sheriff, however, who, on receiving our word that we would give him no trouble, freed us from the disgusting bonds.

"In an instant there was an uproar, some demanding that our chains should be removed, and others swearing that they should not."—Page 154.

This change of our fortune was as sudden as it was unexpected. We enjoyed supper with Captain Smith, having finished which, we found the deputy sheriff ready, with a team of splendid horses, to convey us to his own residence, some two miles from town. We were not long in ascertaining that the sheriff was a Western Virginia man, and that his sympathies were with the United States government. He informed us that Captain Smith was under bonds for ten thousand dollars for his good behavior. From the Captain we got the story of the men who followed us in the sweet-potato patch on the same day we came to the old church, of which I have before spoken.

In the course of their pursuit they had stopped at the Captain's door, and inquired of him if two men, answering our descriptions, had passed that way lately. Thinking at the moment of the old church, and wishing to test their bravery, he informed them that he believed they would find us there. He took care to add, however, that the building was haunted, and that from out of the graves which surrounded it, they would see men rising without heads. One and another at this exclaimed against going on an errand fraught with such danger from spirits, and we were thereby saved from capture, at least at that time.

After hinting to us the sentiments of Captain Smith and himself, the sheriff invited us to his house. It was constructed of rough pine logs, but scrupulously clean and neat in all its arrangements. We also saw his negroes' quarters, and they were nearly as good as his own house. As we passed along on our way to inspect a field of sugar-cane, we were amused to see the slaves peeping at us from behind the corners of their cabins.

Our friend next furnished us with water, soap, towels, and a razor, and going into the sugar-house, we cleaned ourselves. This expression may seem rather strong to delicate ears, but it is the only term which even faintly describes our task. We at once commenced hostilities, scraping rebel mud, wood-ticks, and body-guards from our skins. The contest lasted for over two hours and a half, we proving entirely victorious.

When it was dark, we heard the same old song that we had heard before, when the negroes were coming from their work. As I sauntered down a lane near by, words of prayer fell upon my ears, and a little investigation discovered to me a female slave down on her knees in her lowly hut, asking God to bless and preserve her husband, who was to be parted from her and sold to a new master. What Christian meekness, resignation, and faith in God's power, did this poor creature manifest in her words of petition! and the lines sprang into my mind:

"Christian men have bought and sold me,
Paid my price in paltry gold;
But, though slave they have enrolled me,
Minds are never to be sold."

Her prayer comforted her, and rising from her knees, she began to sing "the song of David."

CHAPTER XII.

Christian Fellowship—Candid Conversation with a Slaveholder—Clay-eaters—A True Unionist—Secret Organizations in the South—Washington and Randolph on Slavery—Aunt Katy—Religion and Republicanism—Proslavery Inexcusable in the North—A Distinguished Abolitionist.

As the words of inspiration came to my ears, I, too, sank on my knees, and poured forth my soul at the mercy-seat. I must have spoken rather loudly, for the next morning, this identical slave woman, while dressing my wounded foot, asked me to what church I belonged. On my telling her, she sprang away quickly, and ran and informed her mistress that I was a minister of their church. The lady immediately came to me, her face wreathed in sweet smiles, and inquired if such was really the case. I told her it was, and had been so since my seventeenth year.

"Oh! sir," she answered, "my husband is a member of that church."

At this moment breakfast was announced, and after the conclusion of the meal, I was requested by both the sheriff and his wife, to lead in prayer. The Lord put words into my mouth, and we had, indeed, a happy time. My host then invited me to take a walk with him, which I did, though my foot gave me considerable pain. We fell immediately to conversation, in the course of which I got a full insight into the real condition of affairs in the Southern Confederacy.

To one of my questions, he answered:

"Yes, sir, the war is the cause of all our misery. You see, for instance, this region of country is adapted only to raising cotton, for the land is too light for sugar-cane or rice. The masses of the people in this particular county are employed in cutting timber, which, being floated down the Ocmulgee to Darien, is sold there, and with the proceeds are obtained the necessaries of life, flour, corn-meal, salt, &c."

"Well," suggested I, "you rich men, at least, will not suffer."

"There, sir, you are much mistaken. We shall suffer heavily; for, though we have farms and plantations, yet we have not hands to work them. And another thing, perhaps, you are not aware of, is, that we have thousands of poor men who live here and there, in their pole-huts, rearing large families on the little crops of cotton and so forth, which they raise on some other man's farm, upon which they have squatted. In the fall they hunt, and thus supply their families with meat and salt; the skins of the animals they take to procure the latter article. So they live, half human, half animal, letting their progeny loose upon us. Of course, many of them must starve now. If they could obtain salt, however, they might live on gophers, which abound in the pine-forests."

Presently, we came in sight of a wretched hut, about which I saw some white children playing. My companion led me thither, with the remark:

"I will show you, sir, a family belonging to the class of which I speak."

Upon reaching the hut, my blood almost chilled at the sight of squalid poverty which I beheld. There stood a family of ten persons; a father—who on account of his age had escaped the conscription—a mother, and eight ragged, filthy children. The ages of the latter, I should judge, ranged from one year up to sixteen. The peculiar color of their complexions struck me very forcibly; it was the same as that of the men composing the first court by which I had been tried. My host gave us a reason for it, that "they laid around so much in the dirt, and *ate so much clay.*" I asked the man himself why he and his family ate clay.

"Cause it's good, I golly!" was the prompt reply.

"Well, how are you getting along?"

"Bad enough," said he, "fur we hain't had a grain o' salt in the house fur more'n four months, only as the sheriff here gins it to us."

"What do you live on, then?" I asked.

"Oh, on gophers and corn-meal, now-a-days. But, I golly! our meal's out, and I don't know what we'll do next."

I got this miserable creature to make me a pair of slippers from old boots, for which I paid him one dollar and fifty cents, in order that he might get some corn-meal, which sold at two dollars and fifty cents per bushel. This money was part of a sum that the sheriff had kindly lent me. Before we took our departure, the lady (?) of the hut gave us her opinion, in no measured terms, of the rascally Yankees.

"Ah, sir," said the sheriff, when we were out of hearing, "if I were to speak the real sentiments of my mind, I should be hung before twenty-four hours. I am a Union man, and when you get back to Ohio, I want you to tell all the friends in our Church that I am so. I have twenty-seven negroes, and a thousand acres of land, and I would let the whole of it go, could I only see the Union restored to what it once was. But this I never expect to behold, for while slavery exists, the Union cannot be preserved. I am in reality an anti-slavery man, and these are my reasons therefor: First, it is a sin in the sight of God; secondly, it is an injury to the slave himself; and thirdly, it is an injury to the white race."

"How so?" asked I.

"Because land worked by slave labor is not worth half so much as when worked by free labor. And, besides, if it were not for slavery, society would be much improved, for the rich and poor, as things are now, are very ignorant."

"How do the rich obtain their wealth?" said I.

"In this way. A man comes here, perhaps, with one female slave, and, in a comparatively short time, he has quite a number of young servants about him. Some of these he sells, and with the proceeds purchases a piece of timber-land. This he has cleared, sells the timber, gets more slaves and another piece of land, and so goes on adding to his wealth continually. He has no education himself, and, three times out of four, gives his children none."

My host further informed me that he himself

had three hundred acres of land in Illinois, and that he had intended to send his son to that State to be educated, but he supposed he would be unable to do so now. He said he had no doubt that this Illinois property would be confiscated. "But," added he, warmly, "I do not care if it is, provided the Union is restored!"

The sentiments expressed by this man astonished me, and I could not forbear asking him the reason why he opposed slavery so earnestly, and yet held in bondage twenty-seven human beings.

"I never bought nor sold a slave in my life!" said he. "You saw that old negress, Kate, this morning; well, she belonged to my wife, as did also her two sisters. These other slaves are all their children. I would have freed them long ago, but they refused to leave me; and I, on the other hand, could not leave them to go North, for I would have been obliged to give security that they would not become a pest and burden to the community, and that I was unable to do. So, you see how the case stands. But I am not alone in my sentiments, sir. There are thirty-five of us within an area of ten miles, who have organized ourselves into a society, and hold regular meetings every two weeks, to oppose the conscription. This is confidential, for I know I can trust you." He spoke of the notice which had been taken by Northern journals of the existence of such societies in the South, and referred to the *disunion* associations in the North. I informed him that the latter, thank God, were few and far between, and could do no harm to the cause.

This gentleman's statement concerning the depreciation of Southern land, brought to my mind the authority of the fathers of our Republic on the subject. John Sinclair had written to Washington concerning the difference of the land in Pennsylvania from that of Virginia and Maryland. Washington's answer was this:

"Because there are in Pennsylvania laws for the gradual *abolition of slavery*, which neither Maryland nor Virginia has at present; but there is nothing more certain than that they must have, and at a period not remote."

The sheriff's statement regarding the liberation of his slaves, was the same as that of John Randolph, Governor of Virginia. The latter said:

"The deplorable error of our ancestors in copying a civil institution from savage Africa, has affixed to their posterity a depressing burden, which nothing but the extraordinary benefits confered by our happy climate could have enabled us to support. We have been far outstripped by States to whom nature has been far less bountiful. It is painful to consider what might have been, under other circumstances, the amount of general wealth in Virginia, or the whole sum of comfortable subsistence and happiness possessed by all her inhabitants."—*Addressed to the Legislature of Virginia,* 1820.

In the course of a conversation I had with the old slave woman, Kate, I said:

"Aunt Katy, if the slaves were to be freed, it would not do you much good, for you are old, and will soon pass into eternity."

"Thank de Lord, sah," she replied, "I am ready to go! But, oh! I wish I could only see my children and grandchildren in hope of freedom! And dar's my husband. You see his massa might sell him, and den I don't think I could live. Dar's no danger of *my* massa selling me, for he's a good man, and he's let me and my children learn to read, and I learned my husband."

"What is the law in Georgia on that point?" I asked.

"God bless you, sah! they'd penitentiary a man for learning a slave to read."

This I had heard before, but never until now did I give it credence. Aunt Katy told me she was sorry we had not struck that town before in our flight, as her son was an operator on the Underground Railroad, and would have insured our escape.

Evening came, and once more did I lead in prayer at family worship. I did so with more assurance and faith than the evening before, for I now thoroughly knew the sheriff's sentiments. Had I not known them, I must confess that my faith in his religion would have been greatly weakened. Do not tell me of republican or mutual rights, or Christianity, when the soul is full of tyranny.

"Are you republicans? away!
'Tis blasphemy the word to say.
You talk of freedom? Out, for shame!
Your lips contaminate the name.
How dare *you* prate of public good,
Your hands besmeared with human blood?
How dare you lift those hands to Heaven,
And ask a hope to be forgiven?
How dare you breathe the wounded air
That wafts to Heaven the negro's prayer?
How dare you tread the conscious earth
That gave mankind an equal birth?
And, while you thus inflict the rod,
How dare you say there is a God,
Who will in justice from the skies,

Hear and avenge his creatures' cries?
'Slaves to be sold!' hark, what a sound!
You give America a wound,
A scar, a stigma of disgrace,
Which you, nor time, can e'er efface;
And prove of nations yet unborn
The curse, the hatred, and the scorn."

The Horrors of Slavery.

There are a few weak-kneed politicians in the North, who think to curry favor with the South at this time, by exclaiming, that "we love slavery, and that the negroes were made for slaves." Did they but know the opinion of Union men in the South, their hopes for popularity would be for ever blighted.

After our devotions were ended, conversation on the current topics of the day was resumed. The sheriff expressed the hope that he would soon hear of the arrests of all in the North who were opposed to a vigorous prosecution of the war. This converse we continued until bed-time, when, again joining in a supplication to the Throne of Grace, we retired for the night. But sleep was a stranger to my eyes, for my foot and hand, although Aunt Katy had dressed them skilfully, gave me excessive pain. As I lay writhing on my couch, I was unable to banish the thoughts that came flashing into my mind concerning the bondmen of the South;

and I pondered deeply whether I could not do something toward benefitting them. Yet when such men as Washington and Jefferson failed, how should I succeed?

"But," exclaims the tender-footed Union man, "you would not intimate that Washington was an abolitionist?"

To such an one I would say, "Hear the words of that great and good man."

"The benevolence of your heart, my dear Marquis, is so conspicuous on all occasions, that I never wonder at fresh proofs of it. But your late purchase of an estate in the colony of Cayenne, with a view of emancipating the slave, is a generous and noble proof of your humanity. Would to God a like spirit might diffuse itself generally among the minds of the people of this country! But I despair of seeing it. Some petitions were presented to the Assembly, at its last session, for the abolition of slavery, but they scarcely obtained a hearing."—*Letter to Lafayette.*

Rising early the next morning, I walked abroad to view the works of God; and as I limped along, I thanked him exceedingly for his goodness and kindness to me, his unworthy servant. As I passed the cabins of the sheriff's slaves, they were preparing to go up to his house for prayers.

After breakfast, our host, taking us aside, informed us that as we had been committed to his charge, he would be obliged to return us to Macon, where he would get the commandant to parole us, limiting us at the same time to the boundaries of the State. Had he himself come across us accidentally, he assured us that, instead of holding us, he would have had us conveyed secretly to our lines. But this, under the circumstances, he was now unable to do, as he would thereby incur the death-penalty himself. We, of course, assented to this, as it would have been extremely ungrateful to our host, who had protected us from violence, to refuse.

CHAPTER XIII.

Classes in the Confederacy—Terror of a Name—Insurrection—Suppressing a Religious Meeting—The Safe Ground—A Sad Parting—Why Prisoners' Stories Differ—Effect of Church Division—The Darien Road—A Wealthy Planter.

DURING the day, I walked out into the pines that I might be alone with my thoughts; and there in the solitude I mused upon all the knowledge that I had gained from my host, and also from my previous experience. Oh! thought I, if our people at the North were permitted to look into the hearts of the better class in the South, there they would see nothing but opposition to the great sin of slavery. Could they but see the South as I have seen it, they would come to the same conclusions as myself, viz., that there are three distinct classes or castes. First, there are the clay-eaters, or common mass of the people, upon whom even the negroes look down with contempt. Second, there is the middle class, in which we find all those who sympathize with the North in this war. Lastly, we have the slave-owning aristocracy, haughty, supercilious and powerful.

Our host belonged to the middle class, and on being questioned why that class held the peculiar position it did in regard to the rebellion, he replied:

"We know that the very moment they—the aristocracy—succeed in forming a Confederacy, they will, of necessity, keep a large standing army. Into this army they will force the sons of the poorest class, or clay-eaters, while they themselves, having negroes to do all their labor, will have full control of affairs. Then assuming all the lucrative offices for themselves, they will force us in reality to support them.

"You may ask why we do not educate the poor whites, and thus set at work a force that would destroy the power of the aristocracy. We would willingly do so, but for the fact that they are so stubborn, ignorant, and bigoted, that any attempt of such a nature would be termed *abolition*, and you might, with far more safety, call a man a thief or murderer than call him an *abolitionist*.

"Should the Confederacy succeed, too, there will be another danger, which will require all the power of the government to combat, and that is the insurrection of the slaves. The latter are, almost to a unit, expecting their liberty by reason of this war, and are at present quietly awaiting such a result. Should it unfortunately turn out, however, that the rebellion succeeds, then they will doubtless strike a blow for themselves; and may Heaven spare me from witnessing the terrible scenes which must follow."

Showing me his hand, which I noticed had been wounded at some former time, the speaker added:

"That wound I received in the following manner. It will serve to show what harsh measures have already been resorted to for preventing any rise of the slaves. I used to allow my servants to hold prayer-meetings sometimes in the house; and on one occasion a patroller came to the house while one of their meetings was in progress, and summarily proceeded to break it up. I interfered, when, turning upon me, he struck me a fearful blow with his weapon, breaking my fingers as you see. I instantly shot him. Since then I have been obliged not to allow the meetings."

In my own mind, I could but compare this noble gentleman to many half-hearted Christians in the North, who would assist in perpetuating the curse of slavery on the ground of policy. Shame on such false Christians and hypocrites! They would call themselves democrats of the nineteenth century. They would say they were on the side of Washington and Adams, and all the fathers. But they are not, for Washington was not in his heart a slaveholder, as the following extract from a letter written by him is sufficient to prove:

"I hope," writes he, "it will not be conceived from these observations that it is in my heart to hold the unhappy people, who are the subject of this letter, in slavery. I can only say, there is not a man living who wishes more sincerely than I do to see a plan adopted for the abolition of it."

Reader, you may, perhaps, complain or disapprove of my digressions from the subject of my own perils and adventures to that of slavery; but, so long as God blesses me with thoughts and words, so long will I continue to strike at the wicked, man-degrading institution, with all my heart, with all my soul, and with all my might. Slavery is the baneful Upas that overshadows our glorious Republic, and its deadly exhalations must in time destroy us, unless we cut it down, tear it out by the roots, and completely annihilate it now and for ever. I, with the great founders of the Republic, hold these to be self-evident truths: "That all men are created free and equal; that they are endowed by their Creator with certain inalienable rights;

that among these are life, liberty, and the pursuit of happiness. That, to secure these rights, governments are instituted among men, deriving their powers from the just consent of the governed," &c.

But to return to my theme. When, after passing through innumerable hardships and perils, being imprisoned in Columbus, Mobile, Montgomery, and Macon, and spending twenty-one weary days in the dismal swamps and pine-woods of Georgia, I reached the home of the sheriff, I, like Paul the apostle, thanked God and took courage.

As soon as practicable we set out for Macon, and while memory holds a place in my being, I can never forget the parting of ourselves and the kind family by whom we had been so befriended.

"Good-bye, gentlemen," said the lady of the house, her eyes suffused with tears; "and should we never meet again on earth, we shall, perhaps, in that better land, where all is love and peace."

There was such a sincerity in the fair speaker's tones, that I could not repress the tears that her words brought to my eyes. The servants, too, clustered around us, and in their intelligent countenances I could discern that they appreciated all that was going on. A final shaking of hands, an adieu, and we were off.

Our buggy bore us quickly out of sight of the house, and I must acknowledge, prisoner as I was, that there was a pang in my heart at the moment. And here a thought suggests itself. The reader has, doubtless, often thought, after reading the various and conflicting accounts of returned prisoners, how strange it was that they could so differ. Now, their treatment depended entirely upon their own conduct, and the class of people among whom the chances of war threw them. It was very rarely that any one expressing his opinions against the Southern system as boldly as I did, met, upon the whole, with such good fortune. Those who fared well were semi-secessionists. I will give a case in point:

At Columbus, Mississippi, there was a man from Illinois, who stated that he was a quarter-master in a cavalry regiment. He was an ardent pro-slavery man, and whenever the subject came up, he defended the right of the South to hold slaves, and became enraged if that right was assailed by any of his companions. This man took the trip with us through Mobile, Montgomery, and Macon, and was continually receiving favors that were denied to the rest. While in Macon, he was appointed prison quarter-master; was permitted to run at large, and he used the privilege to post the secessionists in everything that was favorable to them. This man will be referred to again ere I close this narrative.

We were to go by land to Hockinsville, where we were to take the cars. We traveled slowly, in order, as the sheriff remarked, that we might really see the destitute condition of the country through which we passed. We stopped at a place where a deer had just been killed, and obtained some fresh venison. The man from whom we got the meat, was from Eastern Maryland, and, while conversing with him, I found that he had some knowledge of the disunion men of the Methodist Episcopal Church. He was deeply opposed to the separation, but at the same time, candidly admitted that the North had sufficient cause therefor. Still he thought that it would have been far better to remain united, and endeavor to reform the proslavery portion.

"I and this gentleman," said he, turning to the sheriff, "have stood up for our faith comparatively alone, until the outbreak of the war. Since that, we have been joined by several more, but we are crushed, and dare not speak what we think. If we did, we should be hung to the first tree that could hold us."

He persistently contended that it was a very unfortunate thing that the Church had divided, urging that it led to a division of the government. I held not much further argument with him on this subject, as anti-slavery men of his class were very unpopular in Ohio when I left there.

At evening we seated ourselves on the porch of this man's cottage, and began conversing with the family, the subject being changed of course.

The majority of the residents in this county held the same opinions as these two. I would like to give the names of these gentlemen, but as they might possibly get into some of those traitorous Northern papers which circulate in the South, and thereby bring them into trouble, I am constrained to suppress them.

We remained at this house all night, and bidding our new friends farewell, started the next morning on our way. We kept the Darien road, which I could recognize by the descriptions given of it by the negroes. Our next stopping-place was far from agreeable, for every one in it was a strong secessionist—so strong indeed, that, when they found out our characters, They did not object to the sheriff having anything he wanted, but not with us. The keeper they utterly refused to give us anything to eat. of the house at which we were, cursed fearfully, swearing that the d——d Yankees shouldn't have a morsel of food. The sheriff, however, pacified him at last by telling him that I was from Virginia, and that, although I was in the Yankee army, still I was as pro-slavery a man as himself. This made matters a little better, and the surly host proceeded to question me. I baffled him, however, by saying:

"What paper do you take?"

"We don't take none," said he, "fur I can't read. Have you ever been in a fight?" he quickly added to his reply. I answered in the affirmative.

"Have you ever seed a gunboat?"

"Yes," I rejoined.

He then became much interested, and was not satisfied until I had given him a long description of a gunboat, its object, and its powers.

At this juncture five villanous-looking men entered the room, and calling to my listener, took him outside. When the sheriff saw this, he turned rather pale, fearing that some violence was threatened. When he was about to leave with us, he asked the landlord what his bill was.

"Oh, nothing! as you're taking them d——d Yankees to justice," was the reply.

Though by no means complimentary, this expression took a heavy load off our minds, and we were comparatively light-hearted when we took our departure.

The sheriff resolved not to halt again until he reached a place where he was known, as he feared that otherwise we might be mobbed. By rapid driving he reached this point. Drawing up before the door of a tavern, we immediately dismounted, and were invited to enter by a house-servant, who led us to a small fire at which we might warm ourselves. As we sat there, a hard-looking female came in, and seeing my hand bound up, asked me what ailed it. I responded that I had caught cold in an old bruise which had assumed somewhat the character of a felon. She inquired if she could do anything for it. I thanked her, and told her that I had a poultice of sweet gum on it.

We were presently shown up to our chamber, and went to bed. My hand pained me so much, however, that I could not sleep; and getting up, I took a pan of water, and putting into it a lump of opium, which I obtained from my comrade, I laid my hand in it, and so passed the remainder of the night.

We resumed our journey at an early hour, and pressed forward in order to reach the railroad, which was not quite finished to Hockinsville. On the road we were compelled to stop at the house of a man named Phillips. He was very wealthy, owning over two hundred and seventy-five slaves, and a fine plantation. He was a bitter and unrelenting secessionist, and therefore the sheriff thought it best not to mention what or who we were. Our horses were put up, and we entered the dwelling. Phillips came in almost immediately after, and opened a conversation about the war. The sheriff inquired of him if he had any late papers.

"I don't take no papers!" he rejoined; "I can't read. But," added he, casting a glance at us, "there was some men hunting round here the other day for them Yankees that got away at Macon, and I only wish they'd catch the thieves, and shoot them!"

This was not pleasant to our ears, and the disagreeable sensation was considerably increased, as Phillips, nodding his head towards us, asked the sheriff his errand to Macon with us.

Our friend hesitated a moment to reply, but finally stated his mission. Phillips instantly flew into a rage, and commenced to swear and threaten dreadfully. The sheriff told him that

I was a Virginian, and of like sentiments with himself, and so forth, but it did not effect much. Phillips spoke of the outrageous conduct of our men, and Butler's famous New Orleans Proclamation, and swore, with a horrid oath, that if he had his own way, he would shoot every Yankee that was caught. I rose, and walked outside, and was followed by Phillips, who seemed fearful of trusting me near the negroes who were hanging round the house, and in whose faces I could see an expression that showed they fully comprehended who we were.

Presently the sound of the approaching train came gratefully to our ears. When it arrived, however, we learned that it would make a stop of an hour, as a number of conscripts were to be put aboard. Fearing to remain longer in Phillips's house, we adjourned into the neighboring pines to avoid the mob. One after another, several wagons, loaded with conscripts, drove up. These conscripts and their friends had, by some means or other, heard of our arrest, but did not know that we were the men. They spoke favorably of us, however, and were heartily endorsed by some old ladies who had come hither with their sons, and who were decidedly opposed to the conscription.

CHAPTER XIV.

On the Cars—An Old Acquaintance—His Reasons for being in the Army—Meeting the Slave we Chased—Rebel Account of our Pursuit—Interesting Advertisement—In Jail Again—Captain Clay Crawford—Prison Fare—Rebel Barbarities—Taking Comfort.

IN due time we took our places on the train, and recommenced our journey. At the next stopping-place, a man in rebel uniform approached me, and said:

"I think I know you, sir."

I made no reply, supposing his object was merely to quarrel with me. He repeated his remark, and still I refused to notice him. The third time he spoke, he said:

"Your name is Rev. J. J. Geer, and you come from Cincinnati, Ohio. You used to preach there in the George street Methodist Protestant Church. I am ———, who studied medicine with Dr. Newton of that city."

He extended his hand, and I instantly grasped it, and shook it heartily. I would state his his name; but, for the same reason that I suppress the sheriff's, I must also omit his. Stepping back to where he had set down a basket, my old acquaintance brought me some biscuits and roast chicken. After this welcome gift had been properly attended to, the donor introduced me to his lady, who was a fine, intelligent-looking person. Her husband then taking his s at beside me, we fell into conversation, the chances of being overheard being small, on account of the noise made by the train. Said he to a question of mine:

"I should never have taken any part in this war, could I have helped myself. But when the conscription law was passed, I knew there was no chance for my escaping it, nor could I remove with my family. If I remained, I must go into the army as a private. This I could not endure, and so I obtained an office."

At this moment, the cars suddenly stopped, and an officer attended by a guard, who must have partially overheard the last portion of the speaker's remarks, ordered him to leave me, and take a seat in another part of the car.

Presently, we reached a place where we were detained three hours. While waiting here, the master of that negro whom we chased in the swamp, and whom I have before mentioned as having a basket of corn strapped to his back, stepped aboard of the train. He came forward smiling, and, taking us by the hand, told us what a fierce chase he had had after us. He then asked us if he should call the negro in, and on receiving an affirmative answer, did so.

I asked, with the permission of his master, why he ran from us in the swamp.

"Kase, sah, I thought you wuz Tom Jimmerson, an' he said he'd shoot me if he ever had a chance."

This negro seemed excessively ignorant; but this is a habit with them all, as a general thing, when their masters are present.

"Where in the d——l did you hide," asked the owner of this slave, "when we were after you?"

"Where did you look?" queried I.

"Well," said he, "when the boy came in and told me that he had seen you in the swamp, I went down to the soldiers who were hunting you on the river, and put them on the lookout. Then I returned and started out all the dogs in the neighborhood. One of these, an old hound, that belonged to Tom Brown, never before failed to bring to us his game within a short time after he took the tracks. In two hours, sixteen of us, with the two negroes and the hounds, were after you hot-footed. Not long after we put the dogs on your track, they got confused, and ran my own boy up to the house.

I called them back, and in returning, Brown's old dog struck round a fence, as we thought, on your track. He kept on the branch back of my field, and there crossed and went up the creek, with the whole pack at his heels. We followed after, and found that he crossed the water again, and came down the other side to where he crossed the first time. There the scent was lost, and the dogs gave it up. We hunted round there till nearly night, and not finding any one, went down to the river to guard it. When we got there, the corporal advised me, with six or eight others, to go up the river and take another hunt; but, of course, it brought no good."

My comrade here informed the narrator how we had been lying concealed under the palm-leaves, and watching all their motions, at a distance of not over a hundred yards or so. This astonished him very much; so much so, indeed, that he seemed to doubt it, until Collins repeated to him the identical expressions used on that occasion by himself, his companions, and the soldiers. He then turned to the sheriff, and said with an oath:

"I've hunted bear, and deer, and fox, and never failed; but these Yankees fooled me bad."

The sheriff told him we were Virginians, which seemed to relieve him, as he exclaimed:

"Well, I thought Yankees couldn't have so much pluck."

One fact he was rather curious about, and that was, how we had thrown the bloodhounds off our track so easily. But this knowledge, which had been imparted to us by the negroes, we refused to divulge.

"Well," said he in conclusion, "I wish you a long life; and if I had the say in it, I'd let you go free, for you're none of these d——d Yankees."

At this moment the cars started, and he, bidding us another good-bye, leaped off, and we saw him no more.

Soon after this little incident, my friend, the sheriff, got a paper which he handed to me. In it I noticed an account of the recapture of Captain Clay Crawford, who was in prison with us, and had escaped at the same time, but had been separated from us in the alarm of that occasion. I read also an advertisement of one J. J. Geer, described as follows: "Six feet and three-fourths of an inch in height, black hair, and blue eyes." Lieutenant A. P. Collins was also named, but without any description.

I knew instantly that I had been reported by

the man that I mentioned in the beginning of my narrative as having been a deceiver. He had measured me in Columbus jail, Mississippi, and, as I was in my bare feet at the time, this measurement was short, as by all military standards I always measured six feet two inches.

There were other unpleasant items in this paper, the principal one of which was that in reference to McClellan's retreat from before Richmond.

In due season we arrived at the end of our journey, Macon, Georgia. In conferring with the sheriff on the subject of our future course, I told him it would be best for his own safety to take us to the prison as soon as possible. This he did; and it was but a short time after, that we were again face to face with the tyrant Rylander. He sent us under a guard of four men to our cells, where the jailor came and robbed us of our money. He took also our watches, which until now we had succeeded in carrying. We were then heavily ironed, and left in those filthy cells with only a little straw to lie upon, and this full of odious vermin.

We ascertained that it was true concerning Captain Clay Crawford's recapture. He belonged to a Missouri regiment, and was a genteel, manly comrade, never, like most of his companions, jeering at religion or its advocates. He was a graduate of West Point, and consequently a man well versed in military matters.

Hearing of our return, Captain Crawford, who was confined close to us, made himself known, and a conversation was shortly opened. We learned from him that he had succeeded in making his escape at the same time we did, dressed in a rebel uniform. Going boldly to the Provost Marshal's office, he passed himself off for a Confederate officer, and obtained a pass to Savannah, where he hoped to be able to get aboard a United States gunboat. His knowledge of the South and Southern officers, and the fact that there was a Captain Crawford in the rebel army, assisted him greatly. In one or two places through which he passed, he was in peril from Union sympathizers, who looked upon him as an enemy. In all these localities he found that all the young, able-bodied men had been swept into the army, while the old men who were left behind were very decided Unionists. This I may add was exactly my own experience.

I asked him what fare he got in prison.

"Oh," said he, "nothing but corn-meal and maggots!"

That he stated truth in regard to the food, I had ample proof, when at night a negro brought us some boiled colards, a species of cabbage. He carried it in a dirty-looking bucket, mixed with corn bread, made of meal and water. Producing two tin plates, he put a mess of the colards on each, and then pushed them through the grating of our cell to us. The greens appeared to have been boiled with something like meat, or rather scraps of refuse fat, certainly not fit for anything save soap-grease. On close inspection of the mess, we could see the maggots, which, by way of curiosity, we commenced to pick out. By the time we had picked out half a teaspoonful of large fat ones—not skippers, but maggots—our stomachs, hungry as they were, sickened, and we could not touch the horrid food.

We then examined our haversacks and a pillow-slip that old Aunt Kate had given us. In the latter, as much to our gratification as surprise, we found two fine roasted chickens, and plenty of elegant corn-bread made with molasses. After enjoying this good fare, we knelt and raised our voices in thanks to the Lord, who still watched and guarded us. We felt very happy, and made the misty old prison ring again with our hymns of praise.

The night passed slowly, for my wounded

hand and foot pained me exceedingly. With the return of daylight, conversation with Captain Crawford was resumed, and we learned that in his cell with him was a man named Rowley, who was from Florida. He, like ourselves, had attempted to pass the lines, but was recaptured in the act.

Originally residing in Florida, taking no part in the war, and attending quietly to his own business, he had been suddenly arrested. The circumstances thereof were as follows: "On the night of August 20th, 1861, a party of ruffians surrounded his dwelling, and without the slightest warning, battered in the door, and rushed into his house. So unexpected and so fierce was the attack, that his wife, who was in a delicate condition of health at the time, sank swooning to the floor. The astonished husband, not stopping to defend himself, sprang to the assistance of his wife. While thus engaged, his assailants seized him, and roughly binding his hands behind him, dragged him from the house, and mounted him upon a mule, which they immediately drove off with them. When thus ruthlessly torn from the bosom of his family, he was looking forward with a husband's fond anxiety to the moment which was to make him a father. And now, more than eleven months had passed away, but he had never heard any tidings of his family or property. He owned several slaves. Whether his loving wife had survived the shock she had received on the night in question, or whether the angels of a merciful God had carried her own soul, and that one yet unborn, away to heaven, he did not know.

His captors had taken him to a negro jail, and cast him into a filthy cell, in which he laid for three or four days, eating nor drinking nothing. By this time, they deemed him sufficiently reduced to become subservient to their will. They accordingly took him from his cell, and brought him to a man they styled "Colonel." By this man he was ordered to take a certain oath. Upon his refusal, he was shown a rope that had been used in the execution of four of his neighbors, and he was informed that it was still strong enough to hang him. The man who held the rope strode toward him for the purpose of placing it around his neck. Thus convinced that there was something more than menace meant, he attempted to reason with his brutal captors, informing them that he was so bewildered that he did not comprehend what they wished him to do.

The person called Colonel thereupon ordered

him to be remanded to his cell. The next day, hearing that the Union forces were approaching them, they hurried their poor prisoner to Macon.

This man gave me accounts of the most horrid scenes that he had witnessed. At one period, he said that it was certain death for a man to refuse to volunteer.

Our second day of imprisonment passed dully enough, and indeed it would have been much worse, but for the converse we held with Captain Crawford and Mr. Rowley, whose principal theme was the lightness of their rations. Their allowance of corn-bread, for instance, was a bit about one and a half inches square twice a day. My wounds were exceedingly painful, but I was obliged to suffer on without obtaining any relief. Before I lay down for the night, however, I comforted myself with joining my comrade in singing those beautiful lines—

> "From every stormy wind that blows,
> And every swelling tide of woe,
> There is a calm, a safe retreat;
> 'Tis found beneath the mercy-seat."

God's blessing made us happy, and we could exclaim with faith, "These chains will not always hold us here." How insignificant were our sufferings when compared to those which had been endured by the followers of Christ in ancient times! Again, while on our wretched couches, we sang:

> "My days are gliding swiftly by,
> And I, a pilgrim stranger,
> Would not detain them as they fly—
> These hours of toil and danger."

The next day I penned a letter to Major Rylander, exhorting him, if he had any fear of God before his eyes, or any spark of humanity in his breast, to have me released from my miserable cell, though it were to take me to execution. I committed it to the care of a negro, who was to convey it to the guard, who in turn was to present it to Major Rylander. Whether the latter ever received it, I never knew, but certainly if he did, he never noticed it.

CHAPTER XV.

An Earnest Prayer—What came of it—A Skeptic—Fiend-Stratagem—Reflections and Opinions on the "Peculiar Institution."

NIGHT again found me still suffering, and still a captive. The next day I heard from Captain Crawford that the prayer which I put up that evening to the Throne of Grace was rather eccentric, very strong, and directed specially to the case of our oppressive jailor. I suppose it must have been rather so, for the jailor visited me the next day. His house was in the prison-yard directly opposite my window.

Entering my cell, as I have said, he ordered me to follow him. I did so, not knowing what fate I was about to meet. When out of hearing of my fellow-prisoners, he said:

"Who is that who prays in this prison every night? It is you, I suspect."

"I presume so," replied I, "for it is my habit to pray night and morning; for I am told in the good Book to pray for my enemies, and I apprehend you are one."

"Well, now, there's no use in fooling! Did you pray for the Lord to kill me?"

"No, sir," said I, "I prayed for the Lord to convert you, or else kill you."

"Well, you prayed for them fellows the Bible speaks of," he rejoined, referring to the Apostles Paul and Silas."

"Yes," I answered.

"Well, that's all one tarnal big lie!"

"Why, sir," I inquired, "do you not believe in the Bible?"

"No! I don't believe one tarnal word of it, I don't."

"Then, sir, if you escape the rod of God in this life, you certainly will not in eternity."

"See here, sir," he rejoined angrily, "you had better mind what you say."

"I will speak my mind whenever it pleases me to do so," I said, looking the jailor directly in the eye.

In this strain the conversation continued, till at length he became so enraged, that, pushing me violently back in my cell, he locked me fast to a staple driven into the floor.

While lying thus, a negro came and gazed intently at me, through the bars of the cell door. This he repeated many times during the day, and at night I asked him if he belonged to the jailor.

"No, sah," said he, "I b'long to the richest man in dis county."

"What are you in here for?"

He dropped his voice almost to a whisper, as he replied:

"Two white fellers came to my quarters one night, and got me to go with 'em. Dey had dar faces blacked all ober. Den dey crawled into a winder whar dar wus some white gals, an' de gals dey hollered, an' de two fellers dey runned, an' I runned arter 'em. But I didn't know what they'd done, an' so I stopped, an' de white men what run arter all o' us, cotched me, an' brought me down here. Den dey chained me like you is now, and den de white rascals what had blacked 'emselves, dey runned off right away. But dey won't b'lieve a poor darkey. Now, massa, Tom White, an' he's a white man, seed dem white fellers what blacked dar faces, an' he told so, an' den I was tuk out o' de cell."

Here the poor creature started after the jailor for the performance of some duty.

I was now desirous to know what Captain Crawford's candid opinion was concerning slavery, but the loud tones in which we were forced to talk prevented me, for fear of drawing down some cruel punishment upon us. I conversed on the subject, however, with my comrade, Lieutenant Collins, and we both resolved never to cease its agitation so long as the Lord gave us life, and so long as there remained a single slave on the fair soil of Columbia. Our minds were much strengthened in this resolve by recalling to memory the teachings of Washington, Adams, Monroe, and others. Abigail Adams, the mother of John Quincy Adams, said:

"I wish most sincerely that there was not a slave in the Province."

Benjamin Franklin, whose life was my schoolbook, in an address to the Senate and House of Representatives, said:

"From a persuasion that equal liberty was originally the portion, and is still the birthright, of all men, and influenced by the strong ties of humanity, and the principle of their institution, your memorialists conceive themselves bound to use all justifiable endeavors to loosen the bands of slavery; that you will be pleased to countenance the restoration of liberty to these unhappy men, who alone, in this land of Freedom, are degraded into perpetual bondage, and who, amidst the general joy of surrounding freemen, are groaning in servile subjection; that you will devise means for removing this inconsistency from the character of the American people; that you will promote mercy and justice towards this distressed race; and that you will step to the very verge of the power vested in you, for discouraging every species of traffic in the persons of our fellow-men."—B. F., Pres't (*F. Gazette*, 1790).

During the dreary night I often awoke, and I remember once, when thus arousing, those beautiful lines came into my mind:

"When for the rights of man we fight,
  And all seems lost, and friends have fled,
Remembering in Misfortune's night,
  New glory rests on Virtue's head,
Duty remains, though joy is gone,
  On final good I fix mine eyes;
Distance all fear, and, though alone,
  Stand ready for the sacrifice."

CHAPTER XVI.

The Rebel Reveille—A Horrid Dinner—A Reinforcement of Little Rebels—The Darkie's Explanation—An Exciting Trial—Hope of Release—Retribution—My Old Chains doing good Service.

THE dawn came at last, bringing with it the reveille of the rebel drums, and the yelling of rebel guards. Our rations, however, took a longer time to reach us, for it was not until about eleven o'clock that the negro brought us a mess of the stereotyped greens and corn-bread. A glance into the pan showed us that the maggots had received heavy reinforcements; but so, also, had our hunger gained strength, and we were glad to receive even the repulsive maggots and spoiled-bread, and thank God we fared so well. I could not forbear questioning the negro concerning this outrageous food, and from him I received the following explanation:

The jailor had some time before purchased a lot of meat at a lower figure than it could now be bought for, for the reason that a portion of of it was tainted. The worst of this meat had been thrown aside into a large box used for holding soap grease.

"He tole me, sah," said the negro, to go to dat box and get dat meat, an' when I tole him it stink like de debbil, he swore de tallest kind o' swore, dat I lied, an' fur me to go git it, as it wus plenty good 'nuff for dem d——d Yankees. I'se sorry, sah, but I had to do as massa tole me."

We were satisfied with the poor slave's explanation, and shutting our eyes, demolished our horrid dinner to the last atom, and were still as hungry as ever, for the quantity of the food was as meagre as its quality. As yet I had received no reply to the letter I had sent out by the hands of the negro, to whom I have previously referred. Days and nights passed successively in monotonous misery, and still I beheld the face of no friend save that One which beamed down from above, and supported me in all my trials. Whenever we got the opportunity, we used to question the negroes as to their opinions and ideas concerning the war and slavery. In so doing, we assumed a great risk, as a white man who is caught conversing with the slaves, receives the most rigorous treatment. One day I asked the slave, who brought us our scanty supply of loathsome food, what he thought of the war.

"God bless you, sah," he answered, in the same whispering tones of caution as I myself had used, "I knows all 'bout it, an' all us niggas knows all 'bout it. Why I couldn't tell you half what we knows an' what we says 'mong ourselves, sah!"

"God grant that more light may be sent into the land of the slave, and salvation to the down-trodden inhabitants thereof!" prayed I, as the negro, seeing his master, hurried away from our cell.

Our rest was much disturbed at night by the howling and yelping of a dog, which was doubtless as much ill treated and starved as we were ourselves.

Time rolled on, but still no event occurred to dispel the gloom that surrounded me, until I learned that the man I had met on the cars, and who, it will be remembered, asserted that he had known me in Cincinnati, had arrived in Macon. I learned, also, that he was reporting it about the town, that in Ohio I was possessed of some degree of influence. The faithful slave who told me this added:

"One of you is a-gwine to be taken out, for

I heard de sheriff say that a lot o' people went to the Major, and wanted him to let you out."

This was, of course, like a star of hope in a dark horizon, and day after day I awaited the appearance of some deliverer who should bid me walk forth free. But, alas! it was a delusive dream, for none came, and I was no nearer liberty than ever.

About this time, an occurrence took place which I here record, to show the workings of that pernicious system which is the real root of all our national troubles. I was standing at the bars of my cell, looking out into the prison yard, and saw Woods, the jailor, order the negro, who used to wait on us, to bring him an ax. Upon receiving it, he deliberately broke off the lock of a trunk that belonged to Captain Clay Crawford, and took therefrom a watch and several cards of jewelry. Soon after the darkey brought us our rations, and upon our speaking of the affair, he was quite surprised that we knew of it. He said the trunk was Mr. Crawford's, and smiled knowingly.

Two days after, a party of men came for the trunk, and found it broken open, as I have stated. They, of course, called the jailor to account, and he was fairly implicated in the matter. Without hesitation, however, the vile robber accused the poor negro of having committed the act. Of course the latter denied the charge, and told the whole truth about it. This enraged Woods, and he tied him up to a rough timber cross so that, while his arms were stretched to their utmost extent, his toes barely touched the ground. He then took a heavy whip, with three thongs, and lashed the unfortunate negro until his shirt was actually soaked in blood.

Occasionally the monster ceased a moment, and bade the victim of his brutality to confess to the deed; but with the most heroic fortitude the poor slave refused to comply, and Woods, finding that he could not succeed thus, untied the bleeding man, and threw him into the cell next to our own.

Between us there was only an iron grating, so that we could converse with the negro, and see with our own eyes the horrible treatment to which he had been subjected.

As chance had it, Captain Clay Crawford himself had been a witness of all the proceedings, and upon seeing the negro so unmercifully beaten, he lost his temper, and uttered a torrent of oaths, swearing that he saw the jailor do the deed. As he was regarded, however, as a Yankee, his word had no more effect than the negro's. As I gazed upon the quivering back of that poor, downtrodden African, I exclaimed, in the words of Thomas Pringle:

> "Oh, slavery, though art a bitter draught,
> And twice accursed is thy poisoned bowl,
> Which taints with leprosy the white man's soul!"

In the power of such monsters what might not we expect at their blood-stained hands? There was but one Deliverer for us, as well as the slave, and that deliverer was God, and on Him we cast ourselves, feeling that He was all powerful. Job truly wrote:

"The wicked man travaileth with pain all his days, and the number of years is hidden to the oppressor."

And with equal truth did the prophet exclaim:

"So I returned, and considered all the oppression that is done under the sun, and beheld the tears of such as were oppressed, and they had no comfort. And on the side of the oppressed there was power, but they had no comfort."

Oh, may the hand be stilled in death that would raise itself to defend such a system!

While the jailor was in the midst of his trouble, the star of hope that had arisen on the coming to Macon of my Ohio friend, and then set so suddenly, came up once more, but with more cheering brilliancy this time; for, through the hubbub that he had raised, I was released from my prison cell the very day on which the poor negro, who had been so unmercifully lashed, was to have his trial. I was scarcely fit to be seen, for I was yet clothed in the wretched rags in which I had lived for several months. Yet, notwithstanding this, when I appeared before the Major, whose opinion, since having heard of my real character and position, was wonderfully changed, he began to bow and scrape in his best style.

"Oh, sir," he exclaimed, "I did not know that you were a minister, or I would not have had you put into that cell. And now," added he, "I will give you a parole of the town, and you may report here every morning."

As commissioners had come to terms concerning the exchange of prisoners, the only object that the contemptible Major had in view, was to induce me, upon my return home, to speak well of him and his friends. I must confess that I lost my temper. However, I said nothing, but, called, in very positive tones, for a guard to accompany me to the military prison, which was near at hand. As I was going thither, the thought that the poor negro was to be tried that day for the offence which had been really committed by his master, shot across my mind, and I resolved that I would do my duty in the matter. I instantly returned to the commandant, and asked him to give me a parole of the town. This he forthwith did, as he imagined that I wished to purchase new clothing. He furnished me, also, with two guards with loaded muskets. I then went to the building where the trial was being held. Upon entering the room, I saw the poor, friendless slave, loaded with chains, sitting in the culprit's dock, while the brutal Woods sat confidently near him, fully expecting to have him condemned. When I mildly requested the court to allow me to speak a word in defence of the accused, Woods sprang to his feet, and swore that they would not listen to any d——d Yankee. This brought the owner of the negro to *his* feet, with the exclamation, that I was a white man, and, consequently, entitled to speak. A long debate ensued on this point, which was settled finally in my favor, and I took the stand.

"Gentlemen," I began, "I am a Yankee prisoner. I have been in some three or four of your county jails, and several of your penitentiaries; but still your commandant has confidence in me, and has given a parole of the town, and your surgeon has made statements which prove me to be a man of some little credit at home. If, therefore, I shall find any favor in your eyes, I will make a statement in reference to the matter on trial."

I paused until I was assured by the court that what I had to say would receive credence, and then resumed:

"I saw that man, Woods, who sits here at my right, force the prisoner at the bar to bring him an axe. Upon receiving it, he deliberately broke open the trunk referred to, and took therefrom a watch and a card of jewelry. Subsequently, that he might extort from the prisoner a false acknowledgment of guilt, he tied him up, and beat him most inhumanly."

This brought Woods to his feet once more, livid with rage.

"You don't mean to say that I broke open that trunk, do you, sir?" he ejaculated, shaking at me his clenched fists.

"I do; and you know you did it!" was my prompt reply.

The villain thereupon lost all control of himself, and, drawing a bowie-knife, swore vengeance upon me. I quietly stepped back, and placed myself between the two guards, who, lowering their pieces, prepared to protect me, should my assailant attempt to do me violence.

I then made a statement that my testimony could be corroborated, if necessary, by Captain Clay Crawford himself, and Lieutenant Collins, both officers in the United States army. He quibbled, and protested, and reasoned, and raved alternately; but it was all useless, and when at last I told the minutest particulars about the affair, such as where the negro took the axe from, *et cetera*, he was forced to give in, and was accordingly found guilty, while the poor black fellow was released amid the most tumultuous excitement.

To show that Providence was retributive in this case, I need only state that the crest-fallen culprit was taken from court, placed in the same cell in which I had been incarcerated, was chained with the same irons, slept on the same filthy bed, and I have no doubt was bitten and tormented by the identical little inhabitants of the last, by which I had been long annoyed, so much to his merriment.

Before my time was out, I reported at the jail, and then went over to the military prison, where I had a bone removed from my wounded hand. I then passed in among the prisoners, and while conversing with them, I was obliged to repeat the story of my escape and recapture many times. That night, on account of the pain I suffered, I was unable to sleep, and so I spent the still hours in reflections on my situation, God's mercy and goodness, and on those dear ones at home, who were then, most likely, peacefully slumbering and dreaming of a soldier of the Union, far away in a Southern prison, wounded and weary, and no one even to speak a word of kindness to him.

The next day I heard of many deaths which had occurred during my absence. Quite a number of the names were familiar to me, and my heart was indeed sad. Some of these noble fellows died shouting for God and their country with their last breath. Think of it, reader, and let it awaken your grateful remembrances for the heroic martyrs. They had left pleasant homes, fruitful fields, beloved relations, and cherished friends, to fight and suffer for the Union. And there, in a loathsome prison, without a pillow for their dying heads, without a covering, without proper food, without medicine, without water even to slake their burning tongues, they died, a glorious sacrifice on a glorious altar.

CHAPTER XVII.

Sufferings of Captives—Shooting a Deaf Man—A Terrible Punishment—Arguments on Slavery—Opinions of Celebrated Men—A Sabbath School in Prison—A Loyal Lady —Pennsylvania a Pioneer—Emancipation—Our Prayer-Meetings—Rays of Sunshine.

A LARGE proportion of the prisoners in Macon were nearly naked, and actually were obliged to wrap rags of blankets about themselves to hide their nakedness, and many times, while listening to their stories of wrong and woe, I was moved to tears. Among several harrowing incidents, about this time occurred the shooting of one of our party, a political prisoner, if I remember right, who was deaf. A brutal guard had fired on him because he did not obey some order which he had given, but which of course, the victim did not hear. I saw the poor fellow writhing in his death-agonies. The shot had pierced directly through his bowels, inflicting a horrid and mortal wound.

Another man named Flood, for the offence of coming nearer than ten feet to the guard-lines, was pinned down to the earth. As this punishment is doubtless not understood by a

"The prisoner is thrown to the ground, either face or back down, according to the whim of the punisher, and a number of stakes are driven in the earth around him."—Page 211.

majority of readers, I will describe it. The person subjected to it is thrown to the ground, either face or back down, according to the whim of the punisher, and while held in this position, a number of stakes or wooden pins are driven in the earth around him, in such a manner as to bind him immovably to the ground. A more terrible punishment can scarcely be conceived.

Flood was a large man, and possessed of immense strength; and the first time he was thus pinned down, he tore himself loose from his fastenings. Upon seeing this, his captors again seized him. But he struggled manfully, and it was not until six or eight powerful men attacked him simultaneously, and with weapons, that he was secured. This done, however, they obtained stakes that an ox could not have broken, and with these they fastened their victim down so firmly, that it was impossible for him to move half an inch. And in this position, he lay face down for *twenty-four hours,* during which time a heavy rain fell. In consequence he took a fatal cold, and, four days later, he was laid in the grave. This punishment was quite common among the rebels.

While listening to the accounts of my fellow-prisoners, especially concerning the deaf man and Flood, I could not help thinking bitterly of the thousands in the free North, who, while our country is struggling for existence, are apologizing for the vile system which breeds such monsters as I have been describing. Oh reader, if you would be just to yourself and to God, and not allow your mind to be influenced by the fallacies with which traitors would delude you, you would at once perceive the fountain-spring of all our national troubles to be naught else but slavery. And here, at the expense of interrupting my personal narrative, I have concluded to advance some facts and arguments in support of my conclusions. It is a most common and dangerous fallacy to condemn the emancipation theory of Abraham Lincoln, as the cause of this terrible bloodshed that has been going on for two years past. Now I assume the opposite side of the argument, and find myself supported therein, not only by common sense, but all the teachings of past history.

When the question of immediate abolition was first agitated in England, the friends of slavery were loud in their belief that universal insurrection and bloodshed would follow; and nothing could have taken a stronger hold on the sympathies and fears of the people than these same assertions.

In June, 1793, a civil war occurred between the aristocrats and republicans of St. Domingo, and the planters called in the aid of Great Britain. The opposing party proclaimed freedom to all slaves, and armed them against the British. It is generally supposed that the abolition of slavery in St. Domingo was in consequence of insurrection among the slaves. Nothing is farther from the truth, for the whole measure was nothing more nor less than one of political expediency. A little research into the histories of the island about this period will show that the whole colored population remained faithful to the republicans to whom they owed their liberty.

The British were defeated, and were obliged to evacuate the island; but they still held possession of the ocean, and consequently troubled the French to such an extent, that the latter were entirely unable to look after St. Domingo. The colonists were therefore left to themselves. Certainly here was an opportunity for the breaking forth of that dreaded insurrection which had been predicted as the sure result of immediate abolition. Yet, on the contrary, though there were *five hundred thousand negroes,* thus unfettered and made free, there was an actual decrease in crime, and a corresponding increase in the prosperity and peace of the island.

A resident, Colonel Malenfaut, says in his historical memoir:

"After this public act of emancipation, the negroes remained quiet both in the south and west, and they continued to work upon all the plantations. Even upon those estates which had been abandoned by owners and managers, the negroes continued their labor where there were any agents to guide; and where no white men were left to direct them, they betook themselves to planting provisions. The colony was flourishing. The whites lived happily and in peace upon their estates, and the negroes continued to work for them."

General La Croix, in his memoir, speaking of the same period, writes:

"The colony marched as by enchantment towards its ancient splendor; cultivation prospered, and every day produced perceptible proofs of its progress. This prosperous state of things lasted about eight years, and would probably have continued to this day, had not Bonaparte, at the instigation of the old aristocratic French planters, sent an army to deprive the blacks of the freedom which they had used so well. It was the attempt to restore slavery that produced all the bloody horrors of St. Domingo. Emancipation produced the most blessed effects."

In June, 1794, Victor Hugo, a French republican general, retook the island of Guadaloupe from the British, and immediately proclaimed freedom to all the slaves. They were *thirty-five thousand* in number, and the whites, *thirteen thousand.* No disaster whatever occurred from the humane action of Hugo.

On the 10th of October, 1811, the Chilian Congress decreed that every child born after that date, should be free. Likewise, the congress of Columbia emancipated all slaves who had borne arms in defence of the Republic, and provided for the emancipation, in eighteen years, of the whole slave population, amounting to nine hundred thousand beings.

September, 1829, saw immediate liberty granted by the government of Mexico to every slave in the realm.

Now, in all these cases, not one single insurrection or bloodshed has ever been heard of as resulting from emancipation.

Even the thirty thousand Hottentots—the most ignorant, degraded people on the earth—who were manumitted at Cape Colony, in July,

1823, gave instant evidence of improvement on being admitted to the rights and privileges of freemen. As a gentleman facetiously remarked, they worked far better for Mr. Cash than they had for Mr. Lash.

A statement in the *South African Commercial Advertiser*, of February, 1813, read as follows:

"Three thousand prize negroes have received their freedom—four hundred in one day. But not the least difficulty or disaster occurred. Servants found masters, and masters hired servants; all gained homes, and, at night, scarcely an idler was to be seen. To state that sudden emancipation would create disorder and distress to those you mean to serve, is not reason, but the plea of all men adverse to abolition."

On the 1st of August, 1834, the government of Great Britain emancipated the slaves in all her colonies, of which she had twenty, viz., seventeen in the West Indies, and three in the East Indies. The numerical superiority of the negroes in the West was great. In Jamaica, there were three hundred and thirty-one thousand slaves, and only thirty-seven thousand whites.

Even by the clumsy apprenticeship system, where the stimulus of the whip was removed without being replaced by the stimulus of wages, the negroes were a little improved. They knew they would not be lashed if they did not work, and that if they did work they would not be paid for it. Yet, under such disadvantages as these, there occurred no difficulty, excepting in three of the islands, and even there they were slight and only temporary. Even the bitterest enemies of abolition have not yet been able to show that a single drop of blood has been shed, or a single plantation destroyed, in consequence of emancipation in all the British West Indies!

The journals of Antigua, where the apprenticeship system was not tried, but the stimulus of wages applied at once, say:

"The great doubt is solved, and the highest hopes of the negro's friends are fulfilled. Thirty thousand men have passed from slavery into freedom, not only without the slightest irregularity, but with the solemn and decorous tranquillity of a Sabbath. In Antigua, there are two thousand whites, thirty thousand slaves, and four thousand five hundred free blacks."

Antigua and St. Christopher's are within gunshot of each other, and both are sugar-growing colonies. In the latter island, the proportion of blacks is smaller than in the former, yet St. Christopher's has had some difficulty with the gradual system, while the quiet of

Antigua has not been disturbed for one hour by immediate manumission. Such facts are worth more than volumes of sophistry.

If, however, the humane view be not allowed, let us look at the question in a pecuniary one. The results in this direction, of the British Emancipation Bill, are truly wonderful. To the astonishment of even the most sanguine friends of abolition, the plantations of the colonies are more productive, more easily managed, and accepted as security for higher sums or mortgages, than they ever were under the slave system. It appears from an official statement, that in the first quarter of the present year, there is an increase over the average of the first quarter of the three years preceding emancipation in the great staples of West Indian produce exported, as follows:

From Georgetown, Demarara, twenty per cent. increase. From Berbice, fifty per cent. increase. Coffee increased about one hundred per cent.

The hundred million indemnity thus appears to have been a compensation for having been made richer.

Now, with all this weight of testimony, it is impossible for the candid reader to cleave any longer to the idea that emancipation is the cause of all this misery.

"If," says a distinguished logician, "you have a right to make another man a slave, he has a right to make you a slave." "And if we have no right," says Ramsey, "to sell him, no one has a right to purchase him. If ever negroes, bursting their chains, should come (which Heaven forbid!) on the European coast, to drag whites of both sexes from their families, to chain them, and conduct them to Africa, and mark them with a hot iron; if whites stolen, sold, purchased by criminals, and placed under the guidance of merciless inspectors, were immediately compelled, by the stroke of the whip, to work in a climate injurious to their health, when at the close of each day they could have no other consolation than that of advancing another step to the tomb, no other perspective than to suffer and to die in all the anguish of despair; if devoted to misery and ignominy, they were excluded from all the privileges of society, and declared legally incapable of judicial action, their testimony not admitted against the black class; if, driven from the sidewalks, they were compelled to mingle with the animals in the middle of the street; if a conscription were made to have them lashed in a mass, and their backs, to prevent gangrene, covered with pepper and salt; if the forfeit for killing them were but a trifling sum; if a reward were offered for apprehending those who escaped from slavery; if those who escaped were hunted by a pack of hounds, trained to carnage; if, blaspheming the Divinity, the blacks pretended that by their origin they had permission of heaven to preach passive obedience and resignation to the whites; if greedy, hireling writers published that, for this reason, just reprisals might be exercised against rebellious whites, and that white slaves were happy, more happy than the peasants in the bosom of Africa; in a word, if all the arts of cunning calumny, all the strength and fury of avarice, all the invention of ferocity, were directed against you by a coalition of merchants, priests, kings, soldiers and colonists, what a cry of horror would resound through these countries! To express it, new epithets would be sought. A crowd of writers, and particularly poets, would exhaust their eloquent lamentations, provided, that having nothing to fear, there was something to gain.

"Europeans, reverse this hypothesis, and see what you are. Yes, I repeat it, there is not a vice, not a species of wickedness, of which Europe is not guilty towards negroes, of which

she has not shown them the example. Avenging God! suspend thy thunder, exhaust thy compassion in giving her time and courage to repair, if possible, these horrors and atrocities!"

Now, these things are all perfectly reasonable. Though written a long time ago, they are now not the less true; and those of us who may live to see the end of this war will know well the cause of it; and I trust that the rising generation may profit by the history of their fathers. May they learn from their earliest years to denounce the name that offers an apology for the dark curse of slavery!

It was of this evil that Jefferson spoke in the original Declaration of Independence, drafted by himself, but suppressed by Southern influence. The language is:

"He has waged cruel war against human nature itself, violating its most sacred rights of life and liberty, in the persons of a distant people, who never offended him; capturing them and carrying them into slavery in another hemisphere, or to incur miserable death in their transportation thither. This piratical warfare, the opprobrium of infidel powers, is the warfare of the Christian King of Great Britain. Determined to keep open a market where men should be bought and sold, he has

prostituted his prerogative for suppressing every legislative attempt to prohibit or restrain this execrable commerce. And that this assemblage of horrors might want no fact of distinguished dye, he is now exciting those very people to rise in arms among us, and to purchase that liberty of which he has deprived them, thus paying off former crimes committed against the liberties of one people, with crimes which he urges them to commit against the lives of another."

The same spirit possessed the heart of Luther Martin, when, before the Legislature of Maryland, he delivered a report concerning the topic of which we speak. The report was adopted by a majority of the convention, though not without considerable opposition.

"It was said that we had just assumed a place among independent nations, in consequence of our opposition to the attempts of Great Britain to enslave us. That this opposition was grounded upon the preservation of those rights to which God and nature entitled us, not in particular, but in common with all the rest of mankind. That we had appealed to the Supreme Being for His assistance, as the God of freedom, who could not but approve our efforts to preserve the rights which he had thus im-

parted to all his creatures. That now, when we scarcely had risen from our knees and supplications for his aid and protection, in the form of government we had chosen, we proposed to have a provision therein, not only putting it out of its power to restrain and prevent the slave trade, but actually to encourage that most infamous traffic, by giving the States power and influence in the Union, in proportion as they cruelly and wantonly sported with the rights of their fellow creatures. Such a course ought to be considered a solemn mockery of, and insult to, that God whose protection we had implored, and it could not fail to hold us up to the detestation and contempt of every true friend of liberty in the world. National crimes can only be, and frequently are punished, at least, in the world, by national calamities. And if we thus give national sanction to the slave trade, we justly expose ourselves to the displeasure and vengeance of Him who is equally Lord of all, and who views with equal eye the poor African slave and his American master."

The same fire which dictated the above, burned also in Captain Riley's heart, when he exclaimed:

"Strange as it may seem to the philanthropist, my free and proud-spirited countrymen still hold a million and a half of human beings in the most cruel bonds of slavery, who are kept at hard labor, and, smarting under the lash of inhuman, mercenary drivers, in many instances enduring the miseries of hunger, thirst, imprisonment, cold, nakedness, and even tortures. This is no picture of the imagination. For the honor of human nature, I wish likenesses were nowhere to be found. I myself have witnessed such scenes in different parts of my own country, and the bare recollection of them now chills my blood with horror."

In connection with this, we have the statement of De Witt Clinton, who, during the period of his legislative career—1797—bestowed a large portion of his attention to the protection of the public health, the promotion of agriculture, manufactures, and the arts, the *gradual* abolition of slavery, &c.

The record of the proceedings of the Senate of New York for the sessions of 1809-11 exhibits proofs of Mr. Clinton's great usefulness. Under his auspices, the New York Historical Society was incorporated, the Orphan Asylum and free schools were fostered and encouraged. He introduced laws to prevent kidnapping, and the further introduction of slaves; also to punish those who should treat slaves inhumanly.—*De Witt Clinton's Life in Delaplaine's Repository.*

I have been forced, after honest and serious consideration, to the conclusion, that God, who rules all the affairs of men, is now speaking to the American nation in thunder tones. He is afflicting us for the terrible sin of slavery.

The great fear of those who have fostered this rebellion, is that a true knowledge of God and his word would be instilled into the minds of the people. This is proven by their own arguments. Let us cite one from General Duff Green's favorite strain:

"We are of those who believe that the South has nothing to fear from a servile war. We do not believe that the abolitionists intend, nor could they if they would, to excite the slaves to insurrection. The danger of this is remote. We believe we have most to fear from the organized action upon the consciences and fears of the slaveholders themselves; from the insinuations of their dangerous heresies into our schools and pulpits and our domestic circles. It is only by alarming the consciences of the weak and feeble, and diffusing among our own people a morbid sensibility on the question of slavery, that the abolitionists can accomplish their object. Preparatory to this, they are now laboring to saturate the non-slaveholding States with the belief that slavery is a sin against God; that the national compact involves the non-slaveholders in that sin, and that it is their duty to toil and suffer that our country may be delivered from what they term its blackest stain, its foulest reproach, its deadliest curse."—*Southern Review.*

Such arguments as these blacken the souls of thousands, shut up the avenues of knowledge in the South, and push on the car of slavery until it crushes all liberty beneath its iron wheels.

While I was thus in my old prison a second time, I met with a friend, Rev. William Rogers. During my absence he had organized a Sabbath-school among the prisoners. He had been fortunate enough to obtain, by some means or other, a copy of the Old or New Testament, and from this precious volume he used to read to the captives, who listened to him in alternate groups. Just about the time that Mr. Rogers was producing a good effect by this habit, the school was peremptorily discontinued by the rebels, who feared the dissemination of abolition doctrines, notwithstanding the fact that Rogers was a Southern man.

While here, I made the acquaintance of Dr.

Doke of East Tennessee, and Dr. Fish of Illinois, both of whom were busy day and night ministering to the physical wants and ailments of the prisoners. Medical stores were meagre, and Dr. Doke informed me that to this cause was traceable one-half the deaths that occured.

Mr. Rogers and I, falling into conversation one afternoon, struck upon the question of God's special providence. In this we agreed very well, but on that of slavery we were opposed to each other. He had been all his life an inhabitant of the South, and though he did not fully justify the keeping of slaves, he did not so blindly and bitterly denounce those of an opposite opinion, as Southerners are generally wont to do. But I still pray for God to bless this good divine, as he loves and venerates the Stars and Stripes. He is one of that class who, notwithstanding all the ordinances of secession, cannot give up their affection for the old standard.

Soon after this, we were sent to Atlanta, Georgia, under guard of one lieutenant. This was the first privilege we had yet enjoyed, and we appreciated it accordingly. Along the route the rebels were extremely anxious to converse with us, but we remained decidedly silent, for the least word, inconsiderately spoken, would have placed us at the mercy of a mob, and we well knew what result would follow that. We were often insulted by such expressions as "Yankee thieves," "nigger-stealers," &c.

With no other incidents than these, we reached Atlanta in safety. Here we found a large number of Confederate wounded from Virginia, for whom large tables had been set out, spread with what food and luxuries could be obtained.

As I was still dressed in the ragged Confederate uniform in which I had escaped from prison, a lady hailed me, to know if I was a soldier. Of course, I answered yes, and for a moment hesitated about the rest of my answer; but, thinking any other course might be productive of ill, I added that I was a United States soldier, and of course could not expect to share in a meal set out specially for Confederates. With an assumption of affectation, she turned away, saying:

"Ah, we do not feed Yankees!"

But I noticed her dark eyes closely following me as I limped away through the crowd, and ere I was out of sight, she came hurrying through the latter, as though to speak to some one near me, and she whispered in my ear:

"I am from New York, and I will give you

a cup of coffee. Come around, and I will slip it to you, but you must keep silent."

My heart swelled with emotion as I obeyed this angel woman, and I know the tears dropped on my face, as, with husky tones, I thanked her for the mug of rye coffee and the nice biscuit she placed in my hands.

We remained here long enough to learn that a captain and three Tennesseeans had been hung for their Union sentiments, and to learn also that captives fared very badly. Then we pushed on to Madison, where we were incarcerated in an old factory building, four stories high, and situated in the southeastern portion of the town. It was two o'clock, A. M., when we arrived, and we were immediately locked up in a room entirely destitute of a bed. But still there was such a contrast between it and the old jail in which we had been immured, that we thought it very fine indeed.

We lay down till morning, and when we arose, we found ourselves in company with General Prentiss and General Crittenden, together with two hundred and sixteen other officers of various grades. Here also I met with my old prison companions, Lieutenants Todd, Stokes, Hollingsworth, and Winslow—all clergymen like myself—Lieutenant-Colonel Adams,

20

Majors Crockett, Chandler, McCormick and Studman. I soon formed an agreeable acquaintance with General Prentiss, who was taken prisoner on Sunday, April 6th, 1862, at Shiloh. It had generally been reported that the General had surrendered early in the morning; but this was false, for I now learned that he did not give up until five o'clock in the afternoon, thus holding at least five or six times his own number in check the whole of that dreadful day. Without doubt, history will do the gallant hero justice; for on that bloody field he displayed coolness and heroism seldom equalled, and never excelled.

I found General Prentiss not one of your half-hearted war men, who fight conditionally, but a whole-souled patriot, who would destroy the institution that is the root of the war. He would not see the glorious banner trailed in the dust to uphold a few Southern aristocrats in perpetuating their horrid system of human bondage. His feelings were consonant with those of John Quincy Adams, when that wise man addressed Congress, February 4th, 1843, in the following words:

"Three days since, Mr. Clayton, of Georgia, called that species of population (slaves) the machinery of the South. Now, that machinery has twenty odd representatives in this hall, not elected by the machinery, but by those who own it. And if I should go back to the history of the Government from its foundations, it would be easy to prove that its decisions have been effected in general by less majorities than that. Nay, I might go further, and insist that that very representation has ever been, in fact, the ruling power of this Government.

"The history of the Union has afforded a continual proof that the representation of property, which they enjoy, as well in the election of President and Vice-President of the United States, as upon the floor of the House of Representatives, has secured to the slaveholding States the entire control of the national policy, and almost without exception, the possession of the highest executive office of the Union. Always united in the purpose of regulating the affairs of the whole Union by the standard of the slaveholding interest, their disproportionate numbers in the electoral colleges have enabled them, in ten out of twelve quadrennial elections, to confer the Chief Magistracy upon one of their own citizens. Their suffrages at every election, without exception, have been exclusively confined to a candidate of their own caste."

General Prentiss was kind and affable to all

around him, and among fifteen hundred men of his command with whom I freely conversed, there was not one who did not love and respect him.

Every day found me growing more and more hostile to the slave system; and the actions of the various States against slavery often recurred to my mind, and always produced a pleasurable feeling. Pennsylvania took the lead in this noble race. The Act is to be found in Smith's Laws, Vol. I., p. 493, 1780. It was for the gradual abolishment of slavery, and every word of it should have been printed in letters of gold. This just Act was, for a long course of years, adhered to and perfected until slavery ceased in the State.

In the year 1827, the following open avowal of the State doctrine was made preface to the Act:

"*To prevent certain abuses of the laws relative to fugitives from labor.*

"They ought not to be tolerated in the State of Pennsylvania.

"Above all let us never yield up the right of the free discussion of any evil which may arise in the land or any part of it; convinced that the moment we do so, the bond of the Union is broken. For the Union, a voluntary compact to continue together for certain specified purposes, the instant one portion of it succeeds in imposing terms and dictating conditions upon another not found in the contract, the relation between them changes, and that which was union becomes subjection."—*Message to Pennsylvania Legislature,* 1836.

Had we obeyed these admonitions when it was first attempted to stop our arguments, had we stood up like men and never yielded our rights on this subject, our foes would never have succeeded. Oh, that the united North had stood up like the martyr, Elijah Lovejoy! Said he:

"I know that I have a right fully to speak and publish my sentiments, subject only to the laws of the land for the abuse of that right; and this right was given to me by my Maker, and is solemnly guaranteed to me by the Constitution of the United States and also the State. What I wish to know of you is, whether you will protect me in this right, or whether, as heretofore, I am to be subjected to personal indignity and outrage."

Was this noble man protected? No! He fell into the arms of his brother one day, shot down on the threshold of his own house, by the bullet of a cowardly and fanatical assassin.

General Crittenden, with whom I also become acquainted here, was a slaveholder, yet he did not pretend to endorse the system. Another gentleman, Lieutenant-Colonel Pratt, of Missouri, born and bred in North Carolina, was strongly anti-slavery in his views.

Henry Clay, that peerless statesman, made the following remarks in a speech before a meeting of the Colonization Society:

"As a mere laborer, the slave feels that he toils for his master, and not for himself; that the laws do not recognize his capacity to acquire and hold property, which depends altogether upon the pleasure of his proprietor; and that all the fruits of his exertion are reaped by others. He knows that whether sick or well, in times of scarcity or abundance, his master is bound to provide for him by the all-powerful influence of self-interest. He is generally, therefore, indifferent to the adverse or prosperous fortunes of his master, being contented if he can escape his displeasure or chastisement by a careless and slovenly performance of his duties.

"That labor is best in which the laborer knows that he will receive the profits of his industry, and where his employment depends upon his diligence, and his reward upon his assiduity. He then has every motive to excite him to exertion, and animate him to perseverance. He knows that if he is treated badly, he can exchange his employer. With the proceeds of his toil to his own hands, he distributes it as his pleasure indicates. In a word, he is a free agent, with rights, privileges, and sensibilities. Wherever the option exists to employ, at an equal hire, free or slave labor, the former will always have the preference. It is more capable, more diligent, more faithful, and in every respect more worthy of confidence."

Among the prisoners with whom I was in company, there were ninety-six incarcerated for political offences; that means for conscience' sake. They were mostly from East Tennessee, and they all, with one exception, believed slavery to be the cause of the war. This they often remarked to me, and invariably added that the war would never cease until slavery was destroyed. These opinions were expressed before we heard of the President's proclamation.

"Why, sir," remarked I, to a Tennesseean of wealth and influence, "we are told by men in our country, that if you in the South thought this, you would be a united opposition at once."

"Sir," was the answer, "there are some in the South, now Union men, whom this notion might affect; but the truth is, that you can never restore the Union until you emancipate the slaves. For their masters can use them, both small and great, old and young, as efficiently as you can white men. They make them hoe corn and cotton to feed and clothe soldiers in the field; and here again the females are as useful as the males. If I could see some move made at this system of slavery, I would have some hope. I am myself the owner of ten or twelve slaves, and I would willingly give them all up to see the desired result brought about. Emancipation, sir, is the only hope that the Union men have of a restoration. While you return the slaves to their masters as soon as you take them, there is no hope. You might as well, when you take a rebel soldier prisoner, send him immediately back to his own lines without parole."

My spirits were often depressed, and on one of these occasions I committed all my papers to the care of Captain Stedman, with whom I had formed a friendship in prison, requesting him that, in case I succumbed to my sufferings, he would endeavor to forward them to my wife.

During the daytime, we were permitted the liberty of the prison yard. One day, while walking about, I noticed a cellar, to which entrance was had from the yard. Into this dark cellar I made my way, and prayed to God to remember me in my sore tribulation. Once, when I was making my exit from this retreat in company with a comrade or two who had joined me, I was seen by Captain Stedman, who on learning what we did there, begged us to pray for him. The next night we prayed in our apartment before retiring. This awakened some surprise among the rest of our comrades, some of whom were swearing and others playing cards. The night following, we held a regular prayer-meeting in our cellar, and God blessed us, and made us exceedingly happy. Each evening thereafter found us holding our prayer-meetings, and each evening saw several recruits added to our number. It had been agreed that there was to be no noise, fearing, as we did, that in case there was, we would be discovered by the guards, and a stop put to our proceedings. The rule was faithfully observed until one night, Captain Stedman, receiving a baptism from on high, could not restrain his happiness, but shouted, "Glory to God in the highest," and the shout was taken up by the rest.

Here, we thought, was an end of our meetings, for the guards heard us. But we were agreeably mistaken.

CHAPTER XVIII.

The Slave's Ruse—The Richmond Enquirer—President's Proclamation—A Negro Prayer—A "Big Bug"—A Casibianca—Death of Mr. Eckles—Thoughts and Plans of Escape—Lieutenant Pittenger.

THE next day after this occurrence, as I was walking in the yard, a negro, who worked in the prison, slyly pulled me as I was passing him, and exclaimed in an under-tone:

"All us darkies gwine to be free, yah! yah!"

"What?" asked I, taking care to avoid being seen by the guards.

"Why, all us nigs gwine to be free, yah! yah! gin us yer coat, massa!"

I fully understood this coat business, as the reader must be aware from an explanation previously given, but, as I had no coat myself, I went to Captain McCormick, my messmate, and got his. It very fortunately had a long rip in the right sleeve.

"Here, nigger," cried I, in loud tones, "can't you get this coat mended?"

"Mended!" exclaimed the intelligent fellow, in assumed tones of wrath, intended for the guards. "I wish dar wus no Yankees! dere more bodder den dar wuff! good deal!"

"Go get it mended for him, you black skunk!" exclaimed one of the guard, "and make him pay well for't."

"Dat's jes what dis yere nigger'll do, I golly!"

The coat was taken roughly away by the negro, and returned the next morning, with the rip mended, and a copy of the *Richmond Enquirer, containing the President's Emancipation Proclamation, artfully concealed in the lining!* The paragraph was carefully marked all around, and its perusal gave me the utmost delight. I dared not tell even my most intimate friends how I got this paper, for there were spies among us to report us.

I felt restive under the curb that kept my tongue still, but the thought rose to comfort me, that, though they bound me in the chains of a slave, the day would come when, with the poet, I could sing:

"Oh, Liberty, thou Goddess heavenly bright,
Profuse of bliss, and pregnant with delight,
Eternal pleasures in thy presence reign,
And smiling Plenty leads thy wanton train.
Eased of her load, Subjection grows more light,
And Poverty looks cheerful in thy sight.

Thou mak'st the gloomy face of Nature gay,
Giv'st beauty to the sun, and pleasure to the day.
* * * * * * *
Wrenched the red scourge from proud oppressors' hands,
And broke, curs'd slavery, thy iron bands.
E'en now, e'en now, on yonder western shores,
Weeps pale Despair, and writhing Anguish roars.
E'en now, in Afric's groves, with hideous yell,
Fierce slavery stalks, and slips the dogs of Hell!
From vale to vale the gathering cries rebound,
And sable nations tremble at the sound.
Who right the injured, and reward the brave,
Stretch your strong arms, for ye have power to save!
Throned in the vaulted heart, his dread resort,
Inexorable Conscience holds his court.
With still, small voice, the plots of guilt alarms,
Bares his masked brow, his lifted hand disarms;
But wrapped in night, with terrors all his own,
He speaks in thunders when the deed is done;
Hear him, ye Senates, hear this truth sublime,—
He who allows oppression shares the crime."

That night our prayer-meeting—which was no longer secret—was one of the happiest we ever enjoyed. I found that, like myself, all had heard of the proclamation, and we all reverently thanked God for it. Next to me was an old negro who had been taken prisoner in East Tennessee. He had originally been freed by his master, a wealthy Georgian planter. When this son of Africa prayed, he let himself out in all the power and exuberance of his strong but uneducated mind.

"O, good Lord!" cried he, "don't let off de steam, but put on more steam, O, good Lord! and don't put on de brakes; but run her right up to de fust of January! And den O, good, blessed Lord, my wife'll be free! Tank God! glory! Amen! God send down de power! Amen, and amen!"

As this earnest freedman ceased prayer, I thought of my own white countrymen who were fighting to keep the slave enchained:

> "And we are free—but is there not
> One blot upon our name?
> Is our proud record written fair
> Upon the scroll of fame?
>
> "Our banner floateth by the shore,
> Our flag upon the sea;
> But when the fettered slave is loosed,
> We shall be truly free."

That night I shall never forget, for we took our prayer-meeting up to the second floor. We had gained in strength, and God had shed his blessing on our efforts, so that even the most profane man in our midst, Captain Crawford, was affected. Said he to me one day:

"After such demonstrations as I have witnessed in your prayer-meetings, all the devils in hell could not make me believe there was no reality in religion."

As the rebel authorities were now arresting and imprisoning every man who refused to bear arms for the Confederacy, we had additions made to our numbers every morning. On one occasion, among a crowd that were brought in, was a very large man. He was five feet eight inches high, and weighed *three hundred and eighty pounds.* He was a man of wealth and influence, and after having had innumerable servants to wait upon him, it came rather hard on him to be obliged to get his own place ready to sleep in. I say *place,* for our quarters were entirely innocent of a bed, and if we took turns sleeping on a blanket, we considered ourselves lucky. In the morning he spent some time in rising, for it needed his utmost efforts to get his vast body to an upright position. His exertions ruffled his temper exceedingly, and as the perspiration poured down his face, he muttered to himself over and over again:

"Now, old Henry, you've got yourself in a h—l of a fix, aint you, you d——d old fool!" Notwithstanding, this old man was very gentlemanly in his deportment.

Among a batch that had lately arrived, was a man whom the rebels were endeavoring to force to take the oath of allegiance to the Southern Confederacy. But his wife, who had been confined just after his arrest, fearing that his regard for her condition might induce him to submit to what was demanded, sent her son, who was only eight years old, to tell his father not to take the oath.

This brave little fellow came nearly one hundred miles on his mission, and, when he arrived, the guards refused to admit him. Undaunted, however, by the rebuff, the young hero got close to the picket-fence, and shouted with all his might:

"Pa! pa! don't you swear! Oh, pa, don't you swear! We can get along; I got the lot ploughed to put in the wheat!"

I wished at the time that this scene could be witnessed by the whole North. I feel convinced that in that case no one would raise a cry of indignation at the arrest of traitors who cry for peace, and who thus aid the South in oppressing the really true Union men in that region.

A gentleman by the name of Shaw, was the object of Confederate malice, and on no rational grounds whatever. Hoping to secure a place of refuge for his wife and helpless children, he had, some ten months previous, sought to leave his native State, Virginia, as he knew that the most terrible battles of the war must take place there. On the road he was met and seized by a band of ruffians, who, without the slightest explanation, tore him from the presence of his family, and hurried him away to jail, for disloyalty to the South. The last he had seen of his wife and four little ones was when they stood weeping and wringing their hands on the roadside, as his ruthless captors carried him from their sight. He had never heard tale nor tidings of them since, and what their fate had been he knew not. His case was only one of a thousand others.

> "See the dire victim, torn from social life,
> The shrieking babe, the agonizing wife.
> See! wretch forlorn is dragged by hostile hands
> To distant tyrants, sold on distant lands;
> Transmitted miseries and successive chains,
> The soul-sad heritage, her child obtains.
> E'en this last wretched boon their foes deny,
> To live together, or together die!
> By felon hands, by one relentless stroke,
> See the fond links of feeling Nature broke!
> The fibres twisting round a parent's heart,
> Torn from their grasp, and bleeding as they part!"

This unfortunate man gave me instances of where he had seen his neighbors hung, some until not quite dead, and then taken down to take the oath of allegiance. In case they refused, they were instantly strung up again.

We were so much encouraged in holding our prayer-meetings, that we finally were bold enough to request the privilege of having divine service every Sabbath. This was granted, much to our surprise, and we had the most happy times imaginable. Oh, it was glorious for the soul to bask in that heavenly sunlight which God thus shed upon us in our dreary prison.

About this time, I became acquainted with Simeon B. Eckels. He was very sick, and requested me often to pray for him. Our friendship was as cordial as it was short, for his sickness was unto death. The God who sent his angel to free his apostle Peter, took our sick brother by the hand, and led him from out the noisome prison to the mansions above, where care comes not, and where sickness is not known. He died at half past ten o'clock, P. M., on August 22, 1862. For several days prior to his death, I was constantly by him, and was much gratified with the manifestations he gave of preparation for the future. Brother Eckels gave me the name of the church in Iowa to which he belonged, also the names of his mother and sister, who lived in Ohio. He requested me to visit the latter. His thoughts were centred solely upon heaven and his mother, and in his moments of revival he would often repeat the lines:

> "My mother, at thy holy name,
> Within my bosom is a gush
> Of feeling, which no time can tame,
> And which, for worlds of fame,
> I would not, could not crush."

Brother Eckels's end was indeed one of peace and bright serenity. At his request I preached his funeral sermon the day succeeding his death, from the text, "They that sleep in Jesus will God bring with him."

At the hour appointed for the funeral of the deceased, a negro drove up with a dirty dray, on which we supposed they intended to throw the corpse, and cart it away like some animal's carcass. At this, the Colonel of his regiment, Colonel Shaw, earnestly requested that we might be allowed to bear the body, and thus prevent the insult offered to the dead. This request had the effect of causing the officers to send for a light wagon, and in this was our sleeping brother and comrade soldier carried to his long home, followed by myself and a companion or two. Gentle be his slumbers beneath the sods of Georgia's soil!

Unfortunately, among some other papers, I lost that on which I had taken the address of Mr. Eckels's mother, and have, therefore, as yet, been unable to fulfil my promise to visit her. Nothing would give me more pleasure than to see this dear old lady, and tell her what a glorious death-bed was that of her son. Since my return home, I have frequently heard a sweet song, the words of which picture before me the last hours of Mr. Eckles. How touchingly appropriate to the dying breath of this Christian hero, were the lines:

> "Soon with angels I'll be marching,
> With bright laurels on my brow—
> For my country I have fallen,
> Who will care for mother now?"

Hitherto our spirits had been borne up by the hopes of a speedy exchange; but as day followed day, this fond hope faded, and we began seriously to think of making our escape. A general rise of the prisoners was proposed, which would no doubt have been successful, with perhaps the loss of five or ten of our number. This I did not personally approve of, as I was unable to travel; but still I stated to my fellow captives, that I would put no hindrance in their way if they should decide upon such a course. A sufficient number not being obtained to give this plan any chance of success, it was finally abandoned for some others that promised more success.

I had ascertained the distance to the river, and also, that if we could reach the latter, we could run down it in a skiff. I immediately selected a comrade, broke the intelligence to him, and obtained his consent to make a dash for liberty. We made known our intention to a third one, and he, too, consented to join in the perilous undertaking. The plan of operations was this:

On the first rainy night, we were to go to some Murfreesboro' prisoners, who had blankets, and obtain some of the latter under the pretense of washing them. We then intended to make our way to the fence, and with our knives, cut around the heads of the nails, so that the boards could be easily pulled off. Then filling the places we had cut with sand, we intended to hang the blankets over the fence so as to hide our work. At some subsequent time, when the guards drove us up to our room, we were going to the fence under pretense of getting our blankets, and intended to remain there till all was quiet. Then, tearing off several boards, we were to make an effort to gain our freedom.

All worked well until the night of our final attempt, and then, unfortunately, one of our companions was taken ill. This was the first disappointment. The next wet night that came, we were all well, and started; but, just as we were about to accomplish our purpose, General Prentiss, with several others, made a like attempt, unknown however, to us. Of course, an alarm was immediately raised, and the guards were on the *qui vive.* The General's party, headed by him, dashed back, and hid themselves in the cellar where we used to hold our prayer-meetings, while we reached our own room in safety. A Tennesseean tore up a plank from our floor, and succeeded in getting one, Lieutenant Ward, up out of the cellar beneath; but, ere another could be assisted thus, the guards had captured the fugitives, and marched them out into the yard. A short time afterward, they were brought back into the room in which we were, amid the jokes and laughs of the rest of the prisoners at their non-success.

A few hours after daylight, a guard of fifteen or twenty men marched in and took General Prentiss, Captain Gaddus, Major Ward, and several others into custody. Where they took them we did not know; but, a few days subsequently, I heard through Dolph, the black boy, that they were put into a common jail, and chained to the floor. From the description he gave of it, their condition must indeed have been horrible.

Think of that, all you who sympathize with traitors, and equivocate, if you can, or dare, upon such acts as these! You may say you do not believe such things were done. Let me then refer you to a case, sworn to by one of the sufferers, upon his return home, now Lieutenant William Pittenger, as noble a young man as ever breathed, and formerly associate of Rev. Alexander Clark, in the publication of "*Clark's School Visitor.*" It is from an official report, given before Judge Holt, by order of the Secretary of War:

"An order came for the execution of our seven comrades who had been tried. It was at that time entirely unexpected to us, although at first it would not have been. Sentence of death was read to them, and they were immediately tied, without any time for preparation being allowed them. They were told to bid us farewell, and be quick about it. They were then taken out of the prison, and we could see them from a window, seated in a wagon, and escorted by cavalry. In the course of an hour or so, the cavalry returned without them. That evening,

Captain Farackers, the provost marshal, called upon us. We asked him how our companions had met their fate. He told us, "like brave men." The next day, we conversed with the guards who were guarding us, with one in particular, who described the scenes of the execution. He told us of a speech of one of these men, named Wilson, from my regiment, on the scaffold. He told us, also, that two of the heaviest men had broken the ropes by which they were suspended, and fell to the ground. They afterwards revived, and asked for a drink of water; which being given to them, they requested an hour to prepare for death, and pray before they were again hung up. Their request was refused, and, as soon as the ropes could be re-adjusted, they were compelled to re-ascend the scaffold. The guard told me that Mr. Wilson had spoken very calmly; had told them they were all in the wrong; that they would yet see the time when the old Union would be restored, and the flag of our country would wave over all that region."

CHAPTER XIX.

Just Judgment—General Prentiss in Close Confinement—Northern Peace Men—Bear Story—In the Hospital—Old Aunt Susie—Sold Children—Without Bread, and Satisfied—What our Fathers thought—An Untrammeled Pulpit—Clay-eaters—Commissioners to Washington—Homeward Bound—An Irate Southron—My Yellow Angel—Our Journey—An Accident—Jeff. Davis' Coffin—Don't Know Myself—Safe at Home—Conclusion.

Is it not passing strange that enlightened Americans can be thus so barbarous? It is related of a certain English judge, that a criminal was brought before him, whom, for certain offences, he sentenced to seven years transportation. The prisoner's friends immediately sent a petition to the judge, stating that he was a well-informed man, and if he had an opportunity, might yet be a useful member of society. The judge forthwith sent for the criminal, and thus addressed him:

"I understand, sir, that you are a man of knowledge, and well-informed, and might be a useful member to society. But see what you have done in the face of all your knowledge.

Now, sir, I had intended to give you only seven years; but because you know better, I shall double your term and give you *fourteen years transportation, with hard labor.*" That was a just judge, and before him should the South be tried for the deeds she has committed during this war.

What renders the offence against the noble General Prentiss so much more aggravating, is the fact, that he was thus treated after he had been regularly exchanged. The man for whom he was exchanged, General Price, had been set at liberty, and returned to his family.

What apology the Southerners could offer in this case I know not; but I suppose they might treat the matter in the same light as they do the wrongs inflicted upon the four millions of human beings whom they hold in bondage. Their reply is, when spoken to of their cruelties to their slaves:

"Oh, they're only niggers!"

So, in regard to General Prentiss, they might say:

"Oh, he's only a Yankee abolitionist!"

And shame mantles my brow as I say that there is a class of men in the North, whom this answer would not only satisfy, but actually delight. Thank God that this class is a harmless minority! What a sorry figure they will cut after the war is over, and the rebels thrashed back into the Union! They remind me of an anecdote I once heard, of a man named John Williams. John was a poor, lazy coward himself, while his wife was just the reverse. Moving to a mountainous region in Virginia, they got a little cabin and lot of ground. One day Lucy, his wife, was working in the garden, while John was nursing the baby. Suddenly an old, hungry bear was seen coming down the mountain side, directly toward them. John instantly dropped the child, ran to the cabin, climbed up the ladder into the loft, and pulled the ladder up after him, thus leaving the mother and baby to do the best they could. Lucy, seeing her chance of escape thus cut off, did not wait to scold her cowardly husband, but seizing an ax, went out to meet the bear. As soon as old Bruin came within reach, the courageous mother struck him on the head again and again.

John, as he witnessed this from the loft-window, cried out:

"Quit that, you Lucy; you'll make him madder and madder!"

Lucy paid no attention to John, but continued chopping away at the bear until she killed him.

As the beast fell dead, John breathed somewhat more freely, and called out:

"Lucy, is he dead?"

"Yes."

"Are you sure he's dead, Lucy?"

"Yes! of course he is."

John came down, and going to where the dead bear lay, he looked first at it, and then at his wife, ready, however, to start off on a run should the brute give any signs of life. After thus contemplating matters, he gave his collar a jerk, and exclaimed, proudly:

"Hurrah, Lucy, *we've* killed a big bear! blamed if we ain't!"

So it is with the peace-men of to-day. They cry now loudly for peace, and whine about the unconstitutional arrest of a few tories. And when it is over, and freedom triumphs, *their* coward lips will boast of victories won over the legions of secession. Such are the Vallandigham traitors.

General Prentiss remained in close confinement until October 6th, and during the time he had been absent from our party. I had been taken with a severe illness, which obtained for me admission to a rear room of the prison, which was dignified by the name of a hospital. Here I enjoyed the privilege of drawing my allowance of corn-meal from the commissary, and taking it, or sending it, under guard, out to some one in the town, to have it cooked. I got a slave, called Aunt Susie, belonging to a widow, to attend to mine, and she did it well. I was forbidden to speak to her, however.

One day, Lieutenant Welsh came in with the report that Aunt Susie was having great trouble. I suspected the reason, but kept silent. The next day, feeling well enough, I obtained permission to take my own meal out to get it cooked. As it happened, two black boys were on guard, and one of these only accompanied me. He knew all about Aunt Susie's sorrow, and, as he walked along, he said:

"Don't b'lieve Aunt Susie 'ill be able to do your cookin', sah."

"Why?" asked I.

"Kase she's in heaps o' trouble, sah. You see, de sheriff sold her little boy an' gal t'oder day, an' she's bin cryin' eber since, as though her heart 'ud break."

"Do you think that sale was right?" said I.

"Well, now, I guess I doesn't, sah!" was the quick reply.

"Well, then, why are you in the army that supports such doings?"

"Ah, sah, dey makes me shoulder my gun,

an' dey makes me fire, sah; but dey can't make me shoot low, so as to hit anybody. When I fire, sah, I shoots ober, d'ye understand, sah? I fires, but nobody gits hurt wid my ball, sah!"

"Well, why is it," continued I, "that your masters mix you up with white soldiers? Why don't they put all you blacks into regiments by yourselves?"

"Yah! yah! sah," said the slave, "dey knows 'nuff better dan dat. Dey knows we'd fight t'odder way, if we got togedder. Yes, sah!"

By this time we reached Aunt Susie's cabin, where I found the poor creature sitting on a stool, weeping bitterly. On her lap lay a little boy two years old, while by her knee stood another of four years.

When I entered the cabin, she sprang to her feet in an excited manner; but when she saw myself and guard, she became calmer.

"What is the matter, Aunt Susie?" I asked.

"Oh, sah," she replied, amidst tears and sobs, "I darsen't tell you, sah, for it'll break my poor old heart."

"Oh, yes, come now, Susie, tell me. If I cannot help you, I can at least feel sorry for you."

"Oh, sah, but you are kind to feel sorry for a poor old slave like me. Dey're sold my two dear little children, and dey'll take 'em away to-morrow, and I knows I'll neber see 'em no more 'till I sees 'em up dar, sah—up dar, sah, whar none of us 'll be sold any more."

As Aunt Susie made this reply, she turned her face heavenward, and pointed up with her finger. In her agonized countenance, wet as it was with her sorrowful tears, I read an appeal for the freedom of the slave, stronger and more touching than all the volumes and speeches that have ever been written or made upon the subject.

I could not stand it any longer, and bidding the poor old slave good-bye, I turned away without my bread, for my heart was full. I no longer wondered at the strength of the language used by Ireland's great orator, Daniel O'Connell, when he said:

"The Americans, in their conduct towards the slaves, are traitors to the cause of human liberty, foul detractors of the democratic principles which I have cherished throughout my political life. They are blasphemers of that great and sacred name which they pretend to honor. For in their solemn league and covenant, the Declaration of Independence, they declare that all men have certain 'inalienable rights.' These they defined to be life, liberty, and the pursuit of happiness. To maintain these, they pledged themselves with all the solemnity of an oath in the presence of Almighty God. The aid which they invoked from heaven was awarded to them; but they have violated their awfully solemn compact with the Deity, and set at naught every principle which they profess to hold sacred, by keeping two and a half millions of their fellow-men in bondage. In reprobation of that disgraceful conduct, my humble voice is heard across the waves of the wide Atlantic. Like the thunder-storm in its strength, it careers against the breeze armed with the lightning of Christian truth. And let them seek to repress it as they may; let them murder and assassinate in the true spirit of Lynch law; the storm will rave louder and louder around them till the claims of justice become too strong to be withstood, and the black man will stand up too big for his chains. I hope what I am about to say is not a profanation, but it seems as if the curse of the Almighty has already overtaken them. For the first time in their political history, disgraceful tumults and anarchy have been witnessed in their cities. Blood has been shed without the sanction of the law, and even Sir Robert Peel has been enabled to taunt Americans with gross inconsistency and lawless proceedings. I differ with Sir Robert Peel on many points. On one point, however, I fully agree with him. Let the proud Americans learn that all parties in this country unite in condemnation of their present conduct, and let them also learn that the worst of all aristocracies is that which prevails in America, an aristocracy which has been aptly denominated that of the human skin. The most insufferable pride is that shown by such an aristocracy. I will continue to hurl these taunts across the Atlantic. They will ascend the Mississippi, they will descend the Missouri, and be heard along the banks of the Ohio and Monongahela, till the black man leaps delightedly to express his gratitude to those who have effected his emancipation. And oh! but perhaps it is my pride that dictates this hope, that some black O'Connell may rise among his fellow-slaves, who will cry 'agitate! agitate! agitate!' till the two millions and a half of his fellow-sufferers learn their strength, learn that they *are* two millions and a half! If there is one thing more than another which can excite my hatred, it is the laws which the Americans have framed to prevent the instruction of their slaves. To teach a slave to read is made a capital offence! Shame! To be seen in the company of a slave who can write, is visited with imprisonment! Shame! And to teach the slave the principles of freedom is punishable with death! It may be asked, Are these human laws? Are they not made by the wolves of the forest? No, but they are made by a congregation of two-legged wolves, American wolves, monsters in human shape, who boast of their liberty and of their humanity, while they carry the hearts of tigers within them. With regard to the attacks that have been made upon my countrymen by such men, I rejoice at them. They prove to me that the sufferings to which they have been subjected in the land of their birth have not been lost upon them; but that their kindly affections have been nurtured into strength, and that they have ranged themselves on the side of the oppressed slave."

Would to heaven that ministers of religion, as well as statesmen, would shake off their lip-fetters, and throughout the whole nation proclaim, as with one voice, the liberty of Gospel love! As long as the heralds of salvation are time-servers and caste-courters, there will be Pharisaical hatred to God's poor. The reader will peruse an extract here from a sermon on *Christian Courage*, by Rev. Alexander Clark, delivered in the mid-summer of 1862, some weeks before the announcement of the Emancipation Proclamation. The words are timely and truthful now as then:

"To the Christian citizen, who, in this nation, is greater than a ruler in any other, I would say a word to-day. These are times of sorrow. Our nation is terribly lacerated, and bleeding at every pore. Horrid civil war hangs her black pall over our summer skies. The clouds have hovered long, and still they gather. All the light we have are the vivid lightnings that flash across our battle-fields, though every flash reveals a flying foe, records the victory, and thrills it in electric velocity throughout our loyal land. Then an impenetrable darkness prevails. We cannot yet see the 'cloud with the silver lining.' We cannot hail the day of universal peace. The thick shadows obscure our vision. The groans we hear, and the tears we see, hinder our exulting. Oh, the tears of this war—what a river of them, enough, with the added tears of the suffering slaves for lo! these many years, to float the cruel ship that first brought bondmen to our shores! The graves already filled, and others filling every day, and every where, almost crush our very hopes. In the midst of this darkness and storm, this carnage and blood, we would fear for the result, were it not for the assurance that we feel to nerve us right from the God of nations. *Be not afraid, only believe.*

"And what shall we believe? What shall be our faith? This—no more, and no less—that this nation must first be pure, then peaceable. Amen. Lord, help thou our unbelief! Purify us from all sin! Take away from us all false trust, and all man-glorying! The Lord help us to accept universal liberty for this nation—boldly, immediately, unconditionally, that the sunlight of God's favor may shine upon us once more and for ever! May our rulers and generals, and all Christians, accept the life-thought of freedom to all men as the talisman of triumph henceforth! And may none in authority, may none in the churches or closets, be unwilling to trust in the arm of the Lord. Oh, that the entire people might cease trembling, and *believe,* and be bold for the right!

"The same Power that spoke life to the daughter of Jairus, is able to restore our lost prosperity—is able to return to us our national renown. And He will, if we only believe. Our Republic is young in years, as a child among the nations, but it will yet be raised to its second life, which shall be more glorious than the first. The noise of party politicians and mock mourners shall be hushed as insolence, and the professional fault-finders who ridicule the workings of Providence, shall be *turned out;* and independent of their viperous hisses over a dead Republic, it even already pleaseth Almighty God to awake our slumbering people to the liberty of truth. *His* name, and not a paltry, pitiful *party's*, shall have the glory for a nation redeemed, and a weary, toil-worn race emancipated!

'He has sounded forth the trumpet that shall never call retreat;
He is sifting out the hearts of men before His judgment seat;
Oh, be swift my soul, to answer Him! be jubilant, my feet!
Our God is marching on.'

"And even to-day, while so many are afraid to trust God, afraid to hope that all this commotion shall end gloriously, let us believe that the same Power which conquered devils among the Gadarenes, healed most desperate maladies in the region of His pilgrimage, and raised the cold dead to life again, will give us the great victory.. Brethren, give to the winds your fears!

"A word in view of our national truth. Bless God! in our prosperous North, that has been full and free; and it shall be as enduring as the Plymouth Rock, where it first breasted the New World's winter and storm. That Truth is Christian liberty, unalloyed and untrammeled, the Pilgrim fathers' treasure; that is the citizen-children's inheritance, and it shall be perpetuated. The 'Mayflower' weathered the storms of a December Atlantic. The blood she brought to America courses now in so many veins, and the spirit-life at Plymouth planted, is to-day so thrilling all true Christian hearts, that this strife must end in proclamation of a Gospel to the poor. These we have with us always. Let the people—the *whole* people, have the Truth—the *whole* Truth—and nothing but the Truth. If this include body and conscience-liberty, *be not afraid of that,* and let the good news go forth to captive ones. Truth is used to storms. It has battled and beaten before. Itself bled on Calvary, grappled with Death, and conquered the monster on the marble floor of the new sepulchre, and is to-day a risen Sun of Righteousness, dawning upon the nations!

"The Pilgrim fires, kindled so long ago on the cold New England shores, shall yet dart light and warmth to earth's remotest bounds. America must evangelize the world. But not yet. Not until all human fetters shall have been melted, and all tyranny consumed at home. If it takes fire to purify the people and burn out oppression, then blow, ye winds of heaven, and fan the flames! Let our nation be the land of slaves and sorrow no longer. Give us, O, thou Ruler of men, a home-land of freedom and of Gospel light! Then our missionary efforts will be successful. Then the day of vain mockery at our own pagan idols and wicked worship of the world's trinity, Gold-power-honor, will be for ever ended. Then the true God shall be honored, when His human image is disenthralled, when all hearts and voices publish the good news throughout the land; then shall the high hallelujah melody,

'Sound the loud timbrel o'er Egypt's dark sea—
Jehovah hath triumphed—his people are free!'

ring a joy unspeakable to the benighted sons of heathendom abroad. And the warbling melody, sweeter and richer far than the notes of a bugle-band, shall fill and thrill the very desert airs of Africa. The wild men of Ethiopia shall catch the sounding song, and leap as harts on the mountains. The inhabitants of the far-off sea-islands shall hear the sweet gospel pæan, and welcome a religion that sounds liberty to the captive.

"What music! The first measures of the anthem have been performed in plaintive preludes, outsighing for years, in tedious time, by the weary bondmen of the cotton-fields. Now comes the bold, loud bass, majestic as the march of the whirlwind, introducing the discord of rattling muskets, and anon the rumbling thunder-roar of artillery and the neighing of war-horses. And hark! for an alto, the striking and flashing of swords, the cheers of the victors, the screams of the wounded, and the groans of the dying! But still the sweet ringing melody sounds on high in octaves of glory, like the trill of a freed bird, and as exultant as the angels' song over the Bethlehem hills before the day-dawn; soon the chorus-bar shall be reached and crossed, for the Omnipotent beats the time in downward and upward suns; then the mournful minor strains shall cease, the hoarse bass shall be keyed anew for very joy, and the heavenly soprano of peace, sung by angels and sainted choirs above, shall blend with the glad voices of a freed and shouting multitude in one rapturous burst of accord,

'Sound the loud timbrel o'er Egypt's dark sea—
Jehovah hath triumped—his people are free!'

Who will be afraid, since God rules? *Only believe*, and all will be well.

"Rather let us rejoice aloud and praise the Lord! For now a better day is dawning upon our own dear native land. These sweet summer mornings, with their blessed, balmy breezes, breathe and beam it. The birds warble it. The rain patters it. The flowers nod it. The leaves laugh it. The sun is rising that shall flash it in one blaze of glory the rolling globe around! 'Be not afraid—only believe.' 'Amen; so let it be.' The infamous slave trade, and the scarcely less infamous institution of American slavery, *God is crushing out of this land for ever*—thanks be to His name! Soon our poor shall have the gospel preached to them. Soon shall eyes that have looked so long through tears to a tyrant master's frown, see their prison bands severed in pieces, to fall in tingling music at their feet. Soon shall the illiterate slave be taught to read, in silent meditation, or aloud to his children, the simple story of a Saviour's love. Soon shall the hearts that have sickened at the selling of kindred flesh for gold, bound and beat to the welcome, '*Come*, come unto *me*, all ye that labor and are heavy laden, and *I* will give you rest.'

"The Almighty Deliverer is working now And, as in the days of his incarnation, there are men now who desire in their hearts that God would leave the country. They think Him unable to pay for the loss of the herds. Men will not believe it; but the Almighty Deliverer works. Glory to God! Underneath our cause are the Everlasting Arms; and side by side with the heroic soldier, as he walks to war, the Lord is marching on! Again and again let it ring—let Southern hills the echo sound,

'Sound the loud timbrel o'er Egypt's dark sea—
Jehovah hath triumphed—HIS PEOPLE ARE FREE!'

"Be not afraid to come out, and speak out for freedom. Only believe that the Lord will grant it. Already it comes—the victorious march of the Almighty! The nation's capital He has freed and blessed, and foundationed on consecrated ground. The very flowers must yield a richer fragrance there. The feathered choristers that hop among the elms in the yards and gardens there, so early in the morning, must strike higher, gladder notes of praise. *Now* Washington *is* safe. Let the conquest circle the Republic until the waves of the Gulf and the rippling Rio Grande shall lave the soil of liberty."

Upon my return to prison I found that Aunt Susie's troubles had been heard of there. The little boy and girl played close by the fence during two days,. and then we lost them. They were gone to spend the rest of their lives in chains and slavery, unless the Almighty arm breaks every bond of every oppressor!

I am aware that those who would excuse the slave system, often attempt to give conclusive weight to their arguments by asserting that our forefathers were slaveholders. Let me give some facts to the contrary.

One day, the wife of Samuel Adams returning home from a visit, informed her husband that a dear friend had made her a present of a female slave.

"My dear," replied Mr. Adams, "she may come; but not as a slave, for a slave cannot live in my house. If she comes, she must be free."

She came, and took up her *free* abode with the family of this great champion of American liberty, and there she continued free until her death.

General Kosciusko, by his will, placed in the hands of Mr. Jefferson a sum exceeding twenty thousand dollars, to be laid out in the purchase of young female slaves, who were to be both educated and emancipated. The laws of Virginia prevented the will of Kosciusko from being carried into effect—1820.

A tyrant power had captured nine hundred and twenty Sardinian slaves, of whom General William Eaton thus makes mention:

"Many have died of grief, and others linger out a life less tolerable than death. Alas! remorse seizes my whole soul when I reflect that this is indeed but a copy of the very barbarity which my eyes have seen in my own native country."

"Dissipation, as well as power," wrote the immortal John Randolph, "hardens the heart; but avarice deadens it to every feeling but the thirst for riches. Avarice alone could have produced the slave trade. Avarice alone can, as it does, drive the infernal traffic, and the wretched victims, like so many post-horses, are whipped to death in a small coach. Ambition has its incentives in the pride, pomp, and circumstance of glorious war; but where are the trophies of avarice? The handcuffs, the manacles, and the blood-stained cowhide!"

But to return to my narrative. One morning, as I stood gazing at the guards about our prison, I was forcibly struck with their appearance. They were a new set of men, who had relieved our old guards, the latter having been sent to Richmond. They were all tall and ungainly, and, in speaking, always said "har," "sar," "whar," and "dar." Their most favorite exclamations were, "tarnal Jesus," and "I golly."

As I was thus surveying these degraded creatures, I heard one of them say:

"Tom, what do you always go to old Sanders's mill for? Why don't you go to Mike Adams's mill?"

"Why, you tarnal fool," was the reply, "don't you know there's a good deal better clay up at old Sanders's than there is at Mike Adams's?"

As we were at this time under the charge of one Captain Collins, who was more indulgent than any of our previous keepers, we were allowed to converse with the guards. I resolved to settle this matter of clay-eating. So I asked one of the fellows to whom I have just referred, what his comrade wanted with the clay that he got at the mill.

"Why, tarnal J——s," retorted the repulsive brute, "and don't you know nothin'? He wanted it to eat, I golly!"

Reader, it would be impossible to describe the personal appearance of these wretched clay-eaters, except by the remark an Ohio lady made upon seeing them in all their glory, in Georgia. Said she, "*they do not look like fresh dead men, but men who have been dead some time.*"

Of all the negro-haters in the world, the clay-eater is the most bitter, the cause of which is nothing more than jealousy and a degraded moral system.

While in this prison, we were permitted occasionally to receive our dinners from outside; but even this privilege was stopped every few days, so that it was always altogether uncertain.

Commissioners having been sent to Washington, in relation to the matter of exchanges by cartel, they returned, and brought with them to General Prentiss several hundred dollars, which the General divided among the officers. Our mess, consisting of three, received *one* dollar, which, of course, with prices as high as they were in Dixie at that time, was almost useless. Sometimes we complained of our bad fare, and asked for wheat-bread. Wheat-bread seemed to be a standing joke in rebeldom, or rather one of the institutions that were long since forgotten.

"Wheat-bread indeed!" laughed our keepers, "why poor flour is sixty-nine dollars per barrel!"

On the 7th of October, we left Madison, Georgia, as we hoped, for our homes. Arriving at Augusta, we remained a short time, not being allowed to leave the cars. During our stay, however, we managed to learn from the negroes that there were but few white men in the place.

The loquacity of the darkies gave the guards much trouble; that is, those who were not Unionists themselves, and of the latter class there were many. Captain Collins, whom I have mentioned just before, still had us in his charge, of which we were very glad.

The whites, as well as the negroes, crowded about our cars, and among other questions, we were asked:

"Well, whar did they dun get you? What do you uns tink you uns 'll dun down here? We uns have dun been waiting for you uns."

From this place to Columbia, South Carolina, we were received much in the same manner by all the inhabitants. Thence we took the Charleston railroad to Branchville, from which place, starting due east, we struck the Wilmington road at Kingsville. At Columbia, we were placed for safe-keeping in the State Prison, while arrangements were being made in regard to the cartel. As it was supposed that we would soon be within our own lines, more liberty than usual was allowed us, of which I took advantage by requesting to be allowed to go about the town under guard. My wish was granted.

As I was walking along, I overheard two men talking of a young lady and two gentlemen who had just been put into cells. There was an apple-stand near by, and I stopped, with the apparent intention of purchasing some of the shriveled fruit, but really to listen to the conversation going on between the men.

"I've no doubt," said one, "that they're Yankees."

"Well," said the other, "the lady was put in for hiding and feeding a conscript."

"Yes," savagely rejoined the first, "and if that's so, she ought to have been hung, and not put into prison."

Upon returning to prison, I, in company with my tried friend, Captain Studman, went up stairs, where we both saw the lady and gentlemen in question. She had no hope whatever of escaping execution, and her pale, finely-formed face, though sorrowful, was determined in its expression. Her companions shared her imprisonment, because they had defended her, and to defend such an one was death or imprisonment.

When the appointed time for our departure arrived, we were soon ready. While standing in the street, drawn up in a rank, there was near us an old man, who, whenever he had an opportunity, would grossly insult us. The sun was broiling hot, and my temper, not being much cooler, I felt inclined to admonish this old rebel a little. But, not wishing to offend Captain Collins, who had treated me so well, I refrained, and listened for some time to the hoary-headed coward in silence.

A line of female negroes as long as our own, stood close to us watching us, and commented upon our appearance. While thus engaged, a little dog made his way through them, and commenced barking at, and playing with one of our number, a captain from Missouri.

The captain patted the little animal, and said, in half-joking tones:

"Well, puppy, I've got one friend in South Carolina, anyhow."

At this, the old man rushed up to the prisoner, and exclaimed:

"What are you talking about? Them things 'll hang you before you leave this place!"

"Whom do you think he's talking to, sir?" I asked, in stern tones.

"He's talking to them niggers, and he shall hang for it, before he leaves the place."

Just then, one of our number said sarcastically:

"Ah, now, my dear old gentleman, you are altogether mistaken. He's not talking to your *children*, but your dog!"

This enraged him beyond measure, and he wanted to fight, and demolish the "whole crowd of d——d Yankees at once, and on the spot."

Captain Collins, at length, thinking that he had amused himself long enough, quietly took hold of him, and passed him over to the guards, who, however, were unable to appease him, until they jagged a sharp bayonet into that delicate portion of his corporeal organization, where, doubtless, his feelings and his brains were *seated.*

We were soon after on our way to the capital of North Carolina. On our journey thither, we stopped at Salisbury, where many a Yankee head was thrust out at the car-windows in hopes of attracting the attention of some of the kind-hearted negroes. My unshorn beard and straggling hair, charmed a pretty yellow maiden to such an extent that she drew near and said:

"Are you a Yankee, sah?"

"Yes," replied I, determined to profit by the opportunity, "and I'm a very hungry Yankee!"

"God bless you, sah! I'll go an' git you a possum leg dis minnit."

With these words, she flew away, but soon

returned, bringing a good sized limb of "a possum." I must admit, even at the risk of angering a certain lady, that the yellow angel who thus relieved my hunger, did look very beautiful in my eyes at the time. And as though she read my thoughts, she asked coyly:

"When am you uns coming here for we uns?"

At this moment, a surly, vigilant guard relieved me from the embarrassment which this question produced, and the girl, catching a glimpse of him, "dispersed," without even so much as bidding me farewell.

From this slave girl's question, I was more than ever convinced that the slaves possessed more knowledge of their own rights, situation, and strength, than is generally supposed. I should not be surprised to see them some day rise in one solid phalanx, sweep their masters from existence, and cut their way to freedom! And who could pity the latter? No one. We should be compelled to say just what Mary did to her bashful suitor.

One evening, as the lovers were standing on the verandah, Willie, after immense mental effort, asked his betrothed if he might kiss her. He had never been guilty of the offence before. Mary, delighted that Willie was at last becoming sensible, gave immediate approval. Willie accomplished the kiss, and fainted on the instant. Mary stepped back, and wishing to exonerate herself from any charges which might be brought against her, as to doing him injury, exclaimed loudly:

"You did it yourself! you did it yourself!"

As we traveled to Mason, near the State line, between Virginia and North Carolina, we came to a stream across which was a trestle bridge. Upon reaching the bridge, a rebel soldier who had been standing on the platform of the car, and who was intoxicated, lost his balance and fell through the trestle-work, a distance of full thirty feet. He was seen to fall only by Captain Crawford and myself. He was not missed, however, until we had nearly reached Petersburg, Virginia, where it was discovered when they were about to change guards. This was many miles away from the bridge, and we informed Captain Collins of the accident the moment he came in.

At Petersburg, we fell in with a rebel captain who was one of those fellows who can suit all crowds. He was much animated on the result of the Northern elections, and said that we would now most likely have peace. I asked him why.

"Why," replied he, "look how you are voting over there."

I did not say much, for nothing that could have been said would have done the rebel captain any good, and might perhaps have brought harm to me.

We were obliged to cross the city to reach the Richmond depot, and on our way we passed by a large factory building, in which were confined a large number both of blacks and whites, the negroes for endeavoring to get away, and the whites for their Union sentiments.

During our march to the depot, we were surrounded by a strong guard of cavalry. Oh, how galling it was to me think that I, a native born Virginian, was thus driven through the streets of the principal city of the Old Dominion, without a shoe on my foot, scarcely rags enough to satisfy decency, and soaked by a cold, heavy rain!

At night, we were shut up in an old building that had been used for storing tobacco and molasses. As there were a large number of prisoners here, awaiting exchange, every one was obliged to shift for a resting-place as well as he could. Of course all the best spots were appropriated before our arrival, and we were forced to take up our quarters in the back part of the building. A few of the blankets captured by the rebels at Harper's Ferry were distributed among us; but I, unfortunately, did not get one. So, suffering much from the cold, I laid down in the dirt and molasses, which formed a sort of soft cement of an inch or two in depth. Completely wearied out, however, I soon fell asleep, and dreamed of the happy home in Ohio to which I was going.

The next morning I was roughly aroused by two men who stood on either side of me with barrel-staves.

"What are you doing?" exclaimed I, as the two men began prying me up from the floor.

They did not notice my question, but like sailors weighing anchor, wrenched again at me, exclaiming:

"We'll fetch him clear this poke! heave ho! yo! ho!"

I had positively stuck so fast to the floor, that it was only after the most strenuous exertions I succeeded in getting loose, even with the aid of my two rough helpers.

Our descriptive list did not come until ten o'clock; but when it did, we were not long in signing it, after which we were taken to Aiken's Landing, some fourteen miles southeast of Richmond. Though a cold rain was still falling at intervals, I did not complain, for I was going home,—thank God! home!

Oh, how overflowing was my heart with joy at the prospect! Every drop of rain that pattered on my shivering form, fell upon me like the summer shower falls upon the parched and thirsty grass. I did not complain that I had to march the whole fourteen miles through the cold, mud, and snow, in my bare feet, for I knew that this was my last hardship.

Our guard were not at all rigorous in our marching, and therefore, I often had an opportunity to converse with the teamsters. One of them remarked to me:

"Did you know dere wuz a coffin laid on Massa Jeff Davis's door step t'odder night?"

"No," answered I; "what do you think that was done for?"

"I dunno, I 'spect some ob de Union men done it to let him know dey would kill him if he didn't mind. He's had his house guarded ebber since wid two hundred men."

"Well, uncle, what do you black folks think about this war?"

"Why, God bless you, sah! we been looking for Massa McClellan wid all our eyes. And if he'd jes come leetle closer, dar's a darky here what'ud a leff dis State quick!"

At this instant I chanced to raise my eyes, and there, in the distance, I beheld the glorious old Stars and Stripes floating proudly and beautifully upon the breeze.

"There she is! God bless her stars!" burst from two hundred and sixty throats in one breath of relief. The very clouds seemed to break asunder and let the glorious sun down upon our enfranchised souls. We wept, and laughed, and shook hands, and bounded with delight, until some time after we were taken aboard the Federal transport, which had been sent up the James river for us. We were soon tossing on the ocean, and in due time arrived without accident at Washington.

My first act upon landing and reaching Willard's Hotel, was to secure the services of a photographer, who took myself and comrade with the chain about our necks, and in our rebel rags, exactly as is represented in the engraving. The next important operation was to clean myself, trim my beard and hair, and make myself fit to go into decent society. This was by no means a small undertaking; but by dint of scrub-brushes, soaps of incredible strength, and exercise of muscle to an indefinite extent, I at last succeeded in accomplishing my objects. As I left the bath-room, I noticed at the other end of the hall, a tall strange gentleman, who, for all I did not recognize him, seemed familiar to me. However, I walked toward him, and he did the same, coming toward me. When I got sufficiently near to address him, I bowed and extended my hand. He did exactly the same. I thought he was behaving very strangely, and with rather a grim smile I drew back and raised myself to my full height. He did exactly the same, and I suddenly discovered that I had been the victim of a huge mirror, and that I had, all the while, been mistaking myself for a clever, gentlemanly-looking old friend of mine. I merely relate this circumstance to prove to the reader, that a man who is unfortunate enough to spend six months in Dixie, is scarcely able to recognize himself upon his return home.

Home! home! that word still sounds with strange music in my ears. Its mention brings before my mind the little cottage in Ohio, with its happy yet anxious faces turned up the road, along which papa must come after being away so many months. Home! ah, that is but another name for the dear being, who, while I lay wounded and languishing in the loathsome jails of a merciless enemy, cared for the sweet babes of the captive, who taught their little lips to add a prayer for papa to their vesper offerings at the mercy-seat, and who, weary with many months of watching, never ceased to treasure in her heart's holiest recesses him who pens this tribute.

THE END.

www.ingramcontent.com/pod-product-compliance
Lightning Source LLC
LaVergne TN
LVHW020246110826
845151LV00003B/1032

* 9 7 8 1 4 2 5 5 2 8 3 9 3 *